Offenders with personality disorder

**ROYAL COLLEGE OF PSYCHIATRISTS'
WORKING GROUP ON THE DEFINITION
AND TREATMENT OF SEVERE PERSONALITY
DISORDER**

Offenders with personality disorder

Council Report CR71

Approved by Council: February 1999
Due for review: February 2002

GASKELL

© The Royal College of Psychiatrists 1999.

This report has been approved by a meeting of Council and constitutes official College policy until it is revised or withdrawn. For full details of reports available and how to obtain them, contact the Book Sales Assistant at the Royal College of Psychiatrists, 17 Belgrave Square, London SW1X 8PG (tel. 0171 235 2351, fax 0171 245 1231).

Gaskell is an imprint and registered trade mark of the Royal College of Psychiatrists, 17 Belgrave Square, London SW1X 8PG

The Royal College of Psychiatrists is a registered charity (no. 228636).

British Library Cataloguing-in-Publication Data
A catalogue record for this book is available from the British Library.
ISBN 1-901242-34-X

Distributed in North America
by American Psychiatric Press, Inc.
ISBN 0-88048-967-7

Printed by Henry Ling Ltd, Dorchester, Dorset

Members of the Working Group

Dr Susan Bailey, Consultant Adolescent Forensic Psychiatrist

Dr Derek Chiswick, Consultant Forensic Psychiatrist

Professor Jeremy Coid, Professor of Forensic Psychiatry

Professor John Gunn, Professor of Forensic Psychiatry

Dr Anton Obholzer (Chairman), Consultant Psychiatrist

Dr Michael Shooter, Child and Adolescent Psychiatrist and Registrar, Royal College of Psychiatrists

Dr Peter Snowden, Consultant Forensic Psychiatrist and Chairman of Forensic Psychiatry Section, Royal College of Psychiatrists

Professor Peter Tyrer, Professor of Community Psychiatry

Readers wishing to contact members of the Working Group may write care of The Secretary, The Royal College of Psychiatrists, 17 Belgrave Square, London SW1X 8PG

Contents

1 Definition and classification of personality disorder

Executive summary

Current classifications of personality disorder remain deficient in their theoretical construction and validity. Nevertheless, the adoption of a common approach in the two major international classifications, the International Classification of Diseases (ICD–10; World Health Organization, 1992) and the Diagnostic and Statistical Manual of Mental Disorders (DSM–IV; American Psychiatric Association, 1994), is a considerable advance. There is now an internationally agreed definition of personality disorder, an accepted classification of personality disorder into categories and separate criteria suitable for incorporation into research studies and assessment procedures. Despite these gains, the subject remains in a state of flux and there is an unacceptable degree of overlap between individual diagnostic categories. There will continue to be problems if the term 'psychopathic disorder' is retained as a categorical diagnosis, but it has some use in a research context. There are also problems with the use of the term 'severe personality disorder' unless professionals who use it are explicit in their meaning. The measurement of the severity of personality psychopathology remains unresolved and researchers should endeavour to develop external and objective measures which exclude current diagnostic criteria.

The two major international classifications of mental disorders, ICD–10 (World Health Organization, 1992) and DSM–IV (American Psychiatric Association, 1994), are now very similar in their definition of personality disorder. The ICD–10 defines personality disorders as:

> "Deeply ingrained and enduring patterns, manifesting themselves as inflexible responses to a broad range of personal and social situations. They represent either extreme or significant deviations

from the way the average individual or a given culture perceives, thinks, feels and particularly relates to others. Such behaviour patterns tend to be stable and to encompass multiple domains of behaviour and psychological functioning. They are frequently, but not always, associated with various degrees of subjective distress and problems in social functioning and performance".

The ICD–10 also differentiates personality disorders from personality change:

"they are developmental conditions, which appear in childhood or adolescence and continue into adulthood. They are not secondary to another mental disorder or brain disease, although they may proceed and coexist with other disorders. In contrast personality changes are acquired, usually during adult life, following severe or prolonged stress, extreme environmental deprivation, serious psychiatric disorder, or brain disease or injury".

The ICD–10 goes on to define personality disorder as:

"a severe disturbance in the characterological condition and behavioural tendencies of the individual, usually involving several areas of the personality, and nearly always associated with considerable personal and social disruption. Personality disorder tends to appear in late childhood or adolescence and continues to be manifested into adulthood. It is therefore unlikely that the diagnosis of personality disorder would be appropriate before the age of sixteen or seventeen years".

Personality disorders as conceptualised within the DSM–IV and ICD–10 classifications are derived from psychological trait theory. The DSM–IV defines personality traits as "enduring patterns of perceiving, relating to, and thinking about the environment and oneself but are exhibited in a wide range of social and personal contexts". The diagnostic criteria are described in Box 1.1. Only when personality traits are inflexible and maladaptive and cause significant functional impairment or subjective distress do they constitute personality disorders. The essential feature of a personality disorder is an enduring pattern of inner experience and behaviour that deviates markedly from the expectations of the individual's culture and is manifested in at least two of the following areas: cognition, affectivity, interpersonal functioning or impulse control (criterion (a)). This enduring pattern is inflexible and pervasive across a broad range of personal and social situations (criterion (b)) and leads to clinically significant distress or impairment in social, occupational or other important areas of functioning (criterion (c)). The pattern is stable and of long duration, and its onset can be traced back at least to adolescence or early

Box 1.1 General diagnostic criteria for a personality disorder (DSM–IV)

(a) An enduring pattern of inner experience that deviates markedly from the expectations of the individual's culture. This pattern is manifested in two (or more) of the following areas:
  (i) cognition, that is, ways of perceiving and interpreting self, other people and events;
  (ii) affectivity (i.e. the range, intensity, lability and appropriateness of emotional response);
  (iii) interpersonal functioning;
  (iv) impulse control.

(b) The enduring pattern is inflexible and pervasive across a broad range of personal and social situations.

(c) The enduring pattern leads to clinically significant distress or impairment in social, occupational, or other important areas of functioning.

(d) The pattern is stable and of long duration and its onset can be traced back at least to adolescence or early childhood.

(e) The enduring pattern is not better accounted for as a manifestational consequence of another mental disorder.

(f) The enduring pattern is not due to the direct physiological effects of a substance (e.g. a drug of abuse or a medication) or a general medical condition (e.g. head trauma).

---

adulthood (criterion (d)). The pattern is not better accounted for as a manifestational consequence of another mental disorder (criterion (e)) and is not due to the direct physiological effects of a substance (e.g. a drug of abuse, a medication, exposure to a toxin) or a general medical condition (e.g. head trauma) (criterion (f)).

The ICD–10 also provides diagnostic guidelines which overlap with the criteria of DSM–IV.

Conditions not directly attributable to gross brain damage or disease, or to another psychiatric disorder, meet the following criteria.

(a) Markedly disharmonious attitudes and behaviour, involving usually several areas of functioning; for example, affectivity, arousal, impulse control, ways of perceiving and thinking, and style relating to others.

(b) The abnormal behaviour pattern is enduring, of long standing, and not limited to episodes of mental illness.

(c) The abnormal behaviour pattern is pervasive and clearly maladaptive to a broad range of personal and social situations.

(d) The above manifestations always appear during childhood or adolescence and continue into adulthood.

(e) The disorder leads to considerable personal distress, but this may only become apparent later in its course.

(f) The disorder is usually, but not invariably, associated with significant problems in occupational and social performance.

Both DSM–IV and ICD–10 observe that judgements about personality functioning must take into account the individual's ethnic, cultural and social background. Thus, personality disorder should not be confused with problems associated with acculturation following immigration, or with the expression of habits, customs, or the religious and political values professed by the individual's culture of origin.

Classifications of personality disorder

Table 1.1 lists the diagnostic categories contained within the DSM–IV and ICD–10 classifications. Both ICD–10 and DSM–IV are now considerably closer than in the past and the conditions listed have been agreed by advisors and consultants in different countries as a reasonable basis for defining 'typical' disorders. It is recommended that clinicians should generally record as many diagnoses as necessary to cover the clinical picture, but if recording more than one, the main diagnosis should be specified using ICD–10. For each category in ICD–10, there is a list of criteria and clear evidence is usually required of the presence of at least three of the traits or behaviours given in each clinical description for each category. In DSM–IV there are different thresholds for the number of criteria required for each category. In addition, the DSM system places personality disorders in a different axis of the multi-axial diagnostic system, the second axis. They are therefore commonly referred to as the 'Axis II disorders'. This system is designed to encourage clinicians to diagnose personality disorders in addition to clinical syndromes (in Axis I) and to differentiate between their psychopathology. The DSM–IV system also classifies personality disorder using a clustering system (Clusters A, B and C). These consist of categories that were derived empirically, but which have been supported by factor and cluster analytical studies in normal and personality-disordered populations.

The categories paranoid, schizoid, histrionic, anankastic and obsessive–compulsive, anxious and avoidant and dependent personality disorders are very similar in both classifications. Schizotypal personality disorder is included under Axis II in DSM–IV, but is

TABLE 1.1
Summary of ICD–10 and DSM–IV classifications of personality disorder

ICD–10 (World Health Organization, 1992)	DSM–IV (American Psychiatric Association, 1994)
Cluster A	
F60.0 Paranoid Excessive sensitivity, suspiciousness, preoccupation with conspiratorial explanation of events and persistent tendency to self-reference.	**301.0 Paranoid** Interpretation of people's actions as deliberately demeaning or threatening
F60.1 Schizoid Emotional coldness, detachment, lack of interest in other people, eccentricity and introspective fantasy.	**301.20 Schizoid** Indifference to social relationships and restricted range of emotional experience and expression.
No equivalent	**301.22 Schizotypal** Deficit in inter-personal relatedness with peculiarities of ideation, odd beliefs and thinking, unusual appearance and behaviour.
Cluster B	
F60.2 Dissocial Callous unconcern for others with irresponsibility, irritability and aggression, and incapacity to maintain enduring relationships.	**301.7 Antisocial** Pervasive pattern of disregard for and violation of the rights of others occurring since the age of 15 years.
F60.3 Emotionally unstable Impulsive Inability to control anger, to plan ahead, or to think before acts, with unpredictable mood and quarrelsome behaviour. **Borderline** Impulsivity with uncertainty over self-image, liability to become in-volved in intense and unstable relation-ships, and recurrent threats of self-harm.	**301.83 Borderline** Pervasive instability of mood, interpersonal relationships and self-image associated with marked impulsivity, fear of abandonment, identity disturbance and recurrent suicidal behaviour.
F60.4 Histrionic Self-dramatisation, shallow mood, egocentricity and craving for excitement with persistent manipulative behaviour.	**301.5 Histrionic** Excessive emotionality and attention-seeking, suggestibility and superficiality.
No equivalent.	**301.81 Narcissistic** Pervasive grandiosity, lack of empathy, arrogance, and requirement for excessive admiration.
Cluster C	
F60.5 Anankastic Indecisiveness, doubt, excessive caution, pedantry, rigidity and need to plan in immaculate detail.	**301.4 Obsessive–compulsive** Preoccupation with orderliness, perfectionism and inflexibility that leads to inefficiency.
Dependent Failure to take respon-sibility for actions, with subordination of personal needs to those of others and excessive dependence.	**301.60 Dependent** Persistent dependent and submissive behaviour.
Anxious Persistent tension, self-consciousness, exaggeration of risks and dangers, hypersensitivity to rejection and restricted lifestyle because of insecurity.	**301.82 Avoidant** Pervasive social discomfort, fear of negative evaluation and timidity, with feelings of inadequacy in social situations.

considered among the schizophrenias in ICD–10. Antisocial personality disorder in DSM–IV and dissocial personality disorder in ICD–10 are both categories of considerable importance to offenders with personality disorder. However, these differ in that dissocial personality disorder represents an attempt to define a condition that comes to attention because of its gross disparity between behaviour and prevailing social norms – and is defined by personality traits. Antisocial personality disorder contrasts by defining the condition largely on the basis of behaviours. These must be present both before and after the age of 15 years. The ICD–10 divides emotionally unstable personality disorder into two variants, an impulsive type and a borderline type, whereas DSM–IV retains one category of borderline personality disorder. There is no equivalent to narcissistic personality disorder in the ICD–10 classification.

Alternative concepts of personality disorder

No contemporary diagnostic classification is entirely satisfactory when applied to offenders with personality disorder. The history of psychiatry has demonstrated that the sheer range of psychopathology exhibited by these individuals and its unusual complexity have always posed major challenges to classification (Coid, 1993*a*). Furthermore, there have been confusions over time and conflicts still exist between the different classification systems. It should be remembered that diagnosticians are often prisoners of their time and what is currently the accepted approach may not necessarily be the same in the future. The current ICD–10 and DSM–IV classifications are based primarily (with exceptions such as antisocial personality disorder) on a trait-based system. There are, however, three major approaches to conceptualising the disorders of personality.

Psychodynamic classification

The most widely applied psychodynamic classification groups personality types according to their level of severity and dynamic and biogenic affinities with other diagnostic conditions. This model is derived from Reich's (1949) view, subsequently accepted by many psychoanalysts, that symptomatic disturbances are essentially epiphenomena or secondary extensions of the underlying and more enduring personality disorder. Developments in diagnosis have stemmed from the psychodynamic treatment of patients with character disorder described primarily by Kernberg (1975, 1984) and, to a lesser degree, Kohut (1975). Psychodynamic concepts of borderline and narcissistic personality organisation are most relevant to offender patients and are reflected in the patient's primary characteristics, especially: (a) the degree of identity integration; (b) the type of defensive operation habitually employed; and (c) the capacity for reality testing. Kernberg (1975, 1984) proposed three broad structural organisations – neurotic, borderline and psychotic – which stabilise the mental apparatus, mediating between aetiological factors and direct behavioural manifestations of illness. Narcissistic personality organisation assumes a specific form overlapping with, or in some cases part of, borderline organisation. Offender patients tend to be placed at the most severe end of a spectrum of severity of both borderline and narcissistic personality organisation.

Psychodynamic formulations of offender patients can provide an important alternative framework to explain many clinical observations of the symptoms of offender patients and their behaviour. However, these concepts are not widely adhered to by UK psychiatrists, few of whom are trained in the psychodynamic treatment of patients with character disorder. Furthermore, diagnoses of borderline and narcissistic personality organisation have to be made following a structured clinical interview and much of the psychopathology would not become apparent until the patient had spent some time in psychodynamically oriented therapy.

Cognitive theory

This theory proposes that the dysfunctional feelings and conduct are largely due to the functions of certain 'schemas' (Beck & Freeman, 1990; Davidson & Tyrer, 1996) that tend to produce consistently biased judgements and a concomitant tendency to make cognitive errors in certain types of situation (Beck & Freeman, 1990). Within this theory, schemas are considered to be cognitive structures that organise experience and behaviour. Beliefs and rules represent the content of these schemas and consequently determine the content of an individual's thinking, affect and behaviour. However, the basic premise of this model is that attributional bias, rather than motivational or response bias, is the main source of dysfunctional affect and conduct (Hollon *et al*, 1986), and changes in attribution may be behind successful outcome (Woody *et al*, 1985).

In personality disorders, schemas are considered to operate on a continuous basis in their processing of information and the regulation of cognition, affect, motivation and tendency to action, together with inhibition of behaviour and the directing of the individual's actions. Certain schemas are concerned with the evaluation of others and self. Beck & Freeman (1990) argue that these structures operate in a logical and linear progression from perception through to behaviour. For example, exposure may activate the relevant schema, such as perceiving a situation or person as dangerous (cognitive schema), followed by a subsequent feeling of anxiety (affective schema), followed by a desire to retaliate or carry out some defensive action (motivational schema) and subsequently becoming mobilised to action (action or instrumental schema). If the individual then judges that the action is counterproductive due to external factors, he or she may inhibit the impulse (control schema).

Within this theory, self-directed regulating processes are considered of particular relevance in the case of personality disorders and their behaviour, and these are divided into processes concerned with self-regulation and those involved with relating to the external, primarily social environment. In the case of personality and behavioural disorder in offenders, these individuals are considered to have exaggerated or deficient self-regulating processes.

Cognitive theory has been primarily devoted to devising new approaches to the treatment of psychiatric disorders, including personality disorders, but may have increasing influence on classification in the future.

Trait theory

Trait theory continues to dominate current constructs of personality disorder in the international classifications. This approach traditionally regards personality as the sum of a set of predispositions to behaviours and attitudes that are best recorded as a dimensional structure. A strong body of opinion, most notably that of Livesley and colleagues (Livesley, 1986, 1991; Livesley & Jackson, 1993), regards the dimensional approach as the best form of classification of personality disorders in the forthcoming DSM–V classification, but current classifications include categories. This reflects important differences which separate medical from psychological traditions in their approach to classifying their primary subject domains.

Psychologists have had considerable success in employing methods of dimensional analysis and quantitative differentiation (e.g. intelligence measures, aptitude levels, trait magnitudes, etc.). By contrast, medicine has made its greatest progress by increasing its accuracy in identifying and categorising discrete 'disease' entities. Millon & Davis (1994) have posed the question of whether personality should be conceived and organised as a series of dimensional traits that combine to form a unique profile for each individual, or whether certain central characteristics should be selected to exemplify and categorise personality types found commonly in clinical populations.

The problem with moving to a dimensional classification is that dimensional traits have only recently begun to be taken seriously as an alternative to the more classic categorical approach. Certain trait dimensions have been proposed in the past as relevant to these disorders (e.g. dominance–submission, extroversion–introversion and rigidity–flexibility), but these have not been translated into the full range of personality disorder syndromes. Furthermore, despite their seeming advantages and recent advocates, dimensional systems have not taken strong root in the formal diagnosis of clinical personality patterns. Numerous complications and limitations have been noted in the literature, such as the lack of agreement among dimensional theorists concerning the number of traits necessary to represent personality and psychopathology. There are objections to the use of categories as they contribute to a fallacious belief that syndromes of abnormality are discrete entities, and even medical 'diseases', when in fact they are merely concepts that help focus and coordinate observations.

In practice, there is not a major problem as the current classifications of personality disorder have led to the development of structured clinical instruments which can be used to generate both categorical diagnoses and dimensional scores (see Chapter 2).

'Psychopathic disorder'

Debate continues among psychiatrists on whether to retain the term 'psychopathic disorder' or not. Its use is problematic because it has four contemporary meanings. For example, it can be used by lay persons as a pejorative term or as a term of opprobrium. In the past it has been used as a single diagnostic label and continues to be used within the diagnostic tradition as a research measure of psychopathy using Hare's Psychopathy Checklist (Revised) (PCL–R; Hare, 1991). Its legal use in this country is sometimes confusing for psychiatrists in other countries. It is retained uniquely in England and Wales as a legal category of mental disorder in the English Mental Health Act 1983, where it is defined as:

> "A persistent disorder or disability of mind (whether or not including subnormality of intelligence) which results in abnormally aggressive or seriously irresponsible conduct on the part of the patient, and requires or is susceptible to medical treatment".

For compulsory detention, a proviso is added within the Act that admission is "likely to alleviate or prevent a deterioration of his condition". The treatability qualification means that there should be no obligation to admit patients under the legal category of psychopathic disorder unless it is considered that treatment will be effective.

An alternative use of the term is in the broad generic sense to encompass a wide range of poorly delineated psychopathology exhibited by individuals with severe personality disorder who may exhibit antisocial or other dysfunctional or dissocial behaviours (McCord & McCord, 1964; Coid, 1993). In the diagnostic sense, the problem of defining psychopathic disorder in terms of abnormal behaviour or abnormality of personality is not resolved, despite the emphasis on the latter by contemporary taxonomists.

Psychopathic disorder is not included in ICD–10 or DSM–IV classifications and the use of the legal category has come under increasing criticism. Grounds (1987) has argued that there are doubts about the nature of the disorder, what constitutes treatment, which patients are actually treatable, the effectiveness of treatment and whether evidence of psychological change implies a reduced risk of re-offending. He has argued further that indeterminate hospital orders may provide an unrealistic and unjust framework for the treatment of 'psychopaths' detained in secure psychiatric units. More recently, criticisms have been made of the lack of adequate facilities for the treatment of these patients and the risk to professional and institutional reputations when these patients re-offend (Coid & Cordess, 1992).

In an important review of personality disorder, Rutter (1987) pointed out that three unifying features of personality disorders have been: (a) an onset in childhood or adolescence; (b) long-standing persistence over time without marked remission or relapses; and (c) abnormalities that seem to constitute a basic aspect of the individual's usual functioning. When applied to psychopathic disorder in a generic sense, four additional qualifying features have been applied by Coid (1993a): (d) that it is a particularly severe condition, whether measured according to the number of personality traits, the level of functioning according to a psychodynamic framework or the number of diagnostic labels finally applied; (e) that it is resistant to treatment, as a function either of the severity of the condition or of an unwillingness or lack of cooperation in treatment by the individual concerned; (f) that the abnormality of personality leads to dissocial behaviour (including behaviour harmful to the individual concerned); and (g) that the behaviour may be sufficiently socially unacceptable to lead to formal intervention, such as criminal proceedings, imprisonment and compulsory hospital admission, and can also lead to other forms of social breakdown such as homelessness, vagrancy, etc.

These four additional features do not separate psychopathic disorder from personality disorder but would place it at the far end of a spectrum of severity. However, whether the term psychopathic is still appropriate in modern day usage is debatable. The unresolved problems of lay use as a term of opprobrium and the confusion inherent in retaining the term as a legal category within the Mental Health Act cause major problems and suggest that in most contexts its use should be abandoned.

Definition of severe personality disorder

There is now increasing use of the term severe personality disorder in the context of offenders who demonstrate personality psychopathology. To a large extent, this reflects the increasing reluctance of health care professionals to use the term psychopathic. However, the term severe personality disorder should be adequately defined before it can be recommended for general use. The main problem is that while severity of personality disorder is a central notion to much of the work of forensic psychiatrists, there is no standard way of recording this from the DSM–IV and ICD–10 classifications. It has been noticed in many studies that the patients with more severe personality disorders tend to meet criteria for a greater number of individual types of personality disorder than those with less severe disorders (Kass *et al*, 1985; Oldham *et al*, 1992; Dolan *et al*, 1995).

This, therefore, leads to the suggestion that comorbidity (or, more strictly speaking, overlap) of personality disorder is a measure of severity. There has also been considerable debate about the classification of sub-threshold levels of personality disorder. In the initial draft of the ICD–10 guidelines for personality disorder 'personality accentuation' was included as a category, but was subsequently omitted in the final description. The notion of personality difficulty or accentuation making patients more vulnerable to stresses is a well-established one (Leonhard, 1968) and could have a place in formal classifications. The proposal below combines these approaches and also allows the existing classification systems to be adapted for measuring severity. Five levels of severity of classification are allowed, the first four of which were included in the original description (Tyrer & Johnson, 1996) and the last, or severe category, being added for a special group characterised by 'gross societal disturbance', in which there is gross severity of personality disorder within the flamboyant group and a personality disorder in at least one other cluster also.

Within the current diagnostic classifications there is a problem in deciding whether one personality disorder category is inherently more 'severe' than another (see Table 1.1). For example, if antisocial personality disorder is more prevalent among offender patients, does this automatically indicate that such individuals have a more severe condition than those suffering from paranoid personality disorder? Within a psychodynamic classification there are also levels of severity which are inherent to constructs of personality organisation.

An alternative way of measuring severity would be to apply additional measures, such as those of level of social functioning, needs assessment, seriousness and repetitiveness of offending or other forms of antisocial behaviour, which are not included as criteria.

Recommendations and conclusions

(a) There are clear definitions of personality disorder within the DSM–IV and ICD–10 classifications. We recommend the general diagnostic criteria for personality disorder as summarised in the DSM–IV (see Box 1.1).

(b) Two official classificatory diagnostic systems can be applied to offenders with personality disorder, the ICD–10 and DSM–IV (Table 1.1). We are unable to make a clear recommendation of preference for either system. The official European classification, ICD–10, has not been used empirically with offender populations. It should therefore be made explicit when making diagnoses as to which classification is being used.

(c) The term psychopathic disorder is no longer useful or appropriate as a categorical diagnosis and its continuing use as a legal category is confusing and outdated.

(d) The term severe personality disorder can be defined adequately but has not yet achieved widespread acceptance. Professionals who continue to use it should be explicit in their meaning so as to avoid confusion.

(e) Offenders with personality disorder typically meet criteria for multiple diagnostic categories. This reflects the breadth of their personality psychopathology and, using the criteria for severe personality disorder already mentioned, suggests that most would come into this category.

2 Assessment of personality disorder in offenders

Executive summary

The incorporation of training in the diagnosis of personality disorder into teaching programmes for all psychiatric trainees would significantly raise the quality of assessments of offenders with these conditions. A 'two-dimensional' approach to assessment has been proposed, based on the standard psychiatric interview. This should be incorporated into training in the future. As a minimum, personality disorder categorisation using DSM–IV (American Psychiatric Association, 1994) or ICD–10 (World Health Organization, 1992) classifications should be carried out together with a recognised rating scale in settings for offenders with personality disorder. Risk assessment should also be carried out.

The approach taken by clinicians when carrying out assessments of offenders with personality disorder should be the same as that for offender patients with severe mental illness. A series of problems continues to hamper progress in adopting uniform approaches within different clinical settings in the UK and a general consensus among clinicians still remains elusive. A major problem is the generally negative attitude that many psychiatrists continue to hold towards patients with a diagnosis of personality disorder. Lewis & Appleby (1988) observed that patients with a previous diagnosis of personality disorder were perceived by clinicians as more difficult and less deserving of care compared with control subjects who were not. Individuals with personality disorder tended to be regarded and rated as manipulative, attention-seeking, annoying and in control of their suicidal urges and debts in a study in which case histories were presented to psychiatrists. The authors argued that personality disorder appeared to be an enduring pejorative judgement rather than a clinical diagnosis and proposed that the concept be abandoned. Gunn & Robertson (1976) argued in an earlier study that personality disorder was a derogatory label that may result in therapeutic neglect.

Unfortunately, no alternative system of diagnostic classification which might assist in clinical assessment has been put forward by those who have taken a negative view of psychiatric involvement with these patients. In contrast, North American psychiatrists routinely receive systematic training in the application of the DSM Axis II system of classification. Furthermore, North American diagnosticians have long recognised that a comorbid diagnosis of personality disorder with a clinical syndrome may have considerable significance for the prognosis and treatability of the latter condition.

Routine training in the diagnosis of personality disorder has not been incorporated into teaching programmes for psychiatric trainees. This is the most significant factor leading to poor-quality assessments. It is, therefore, hardly surprising that disagreements continue among psychiatrists on what instruments should be used to make diagnoses and which professionals should carry them out. Coid (1993a) has pointed out that four differing diagnostic systems can be used to classify patients detained under the legal category of psychopathic disorder. Although diagnostic categories derived from a trait-based system are officially adopted by the major diagnostic classifications, it remains unresolved whether the ICD–10 or DSM–IV glossary is more appropriate for offenders with personality disorder. Although the UK is officially aligned with the ICD–10 system, there are few studies of personality disorder categories derived from ICD–10. In practice many UK psychiatrists use DSM Axis II categories. This system was operationalised earlier than ICD–10 and there is considerably more published research to justify its adoption into routine clinical practice with offender patients.

It is clear that training in the diagnosis of personality disorder should now be improved in the UK and that a consensus should be reached on which approaches should be taken on a routine clinical basis. We have discussed the arguments for and against the classification of personality disorder according to diagnostic categories or continuous scores on personality dimensions in Chapter 1 and pointed out that several research diagnostic instruments can be used for both categories and dimensions. We have also observed that most medically trained diagnosticians continue to prefer the categorical approach.

Practical approaches to assessment

Data for personality disorder assessment can be obtained from three main sources: the patient, informants and observation in clinical settings over varying periods. There is evidence that some personality disorders are associated with a higher prevalence of the same, or related, disorders in first-degree relatives and with some biological variables, so that assessment should also include family history and physiological data when available (Reich, 1992). There are three main types of assessment methodology: structured interviews, self-report questionnaires and consensus ratings (or diagnoses) from various sources. The last type includes the standard Longitudinal Expert Evaluation Using All Available Data (LEAD; Skodol *et al*, 1988), which is based on information from patient assessments, past records, informants and observations over a period of in-patient or out-patient contact. In this latter example, the final rating for the diagnosis would be based on the consensus of several experienced clinicians. The process is not dissimilar from clinical assessments that are routinely carried out in secure forensic psychiatry facilities in the UK. However, no matter what procedure is chosen, the reliability of the assessment is likely to be increased by the use of more than one assessment method. Furthermore, informants are often important for personality disorder assessment, in particular where the patient has another mental disorder such as a depressive syndrome or substance misuse, and when the patient is uncooperative.

Zimmerman (1994) has reviewed a range of contemporary research methods and noted that interrater reliability coefficients for the same interview, using standardised interviews, is usually good, in contrast to poor reliability when using unstandardised clinical assessments. This would suggest that there should now be more routine teaching of standardised interviewing techniques to psychiatric trainees. As may be expected, test–re-test reliability coefficients are generally lower than those for joint ratings at the same interview and decrease with increasing time between interviews. However, some personality disorders (such as antisocial) are less affected than other categories over the test–re-test interval. However, co-occurring disorders such as depressed mood tend to influence the results of personality disorder assessment with both self-report questionnaires and structured interviews. Zimmerman has also observed that assessment may be further complicated by a tendency for subjects to report less psychopathology at subsequent interviews. Nevertheless, it must be emphasised that many of these problems can be observed in the diagnostic rating of other clinical syndromes and are by no means unique to the diagnostic assessment of personality disorder.

Guidelines for assessing offenders with personality disorder

Coid (1993*a*) has previously recommended that a comprehensive clinical assessment using a two-dimensional model should be used for patients detained under the legal category of psychopathic disorder. This same model is equally appropriate for offenders with personality disorder and where a subgroup overlaps with individuals legally detained under this category. This model has also been recommended because the literature has demonstrated that three major areas – (a) personality disorder; (b) major mental disorder (clinical syndromes); and (c) behavioural disorder – show considerable overlap in offender patients. No diagnostic system has resolved the problem of comorbidity within or between diagnostic axes, demonstrated the superiority of one trait-based classification or scale over another, successfully separated traits from behaviour, or adequately incorporated a lifetime perspective. A more complex, two-dimensional formulation of offender patients with personality disorder should therefore be employed which incorporates the three elements of personality disorder, mental disorder and behavioural disorder, and with a lifetime perspective taken of each along the second dimension.

This model is illustrated in Fig. 2.1, which shows the two-way interactions between each of these three elements, and reflects the extreme difficulty in separating these overlapping entities. At the same time, the three elements of personality disorder, clinical syndrome and behaviour can change according to the patient's developmental stage. Considerable information is now available on the development of behavioural disorder from infancy to adulthood. Similarly, psychiatric research increasingly provides data on the age of presentation and longitudinal course of clinical syndromes, including major mental disorders, substance misuse, etc. However, despite the contemporary emphasis on a trait-based classification of personality

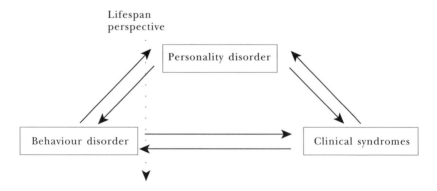

FIG. 2.1   *Two-dimensional approach to assessment*

disorder, little is known of the longitudinal development of personality traits.

In future, a comprehensive clinical assessment of offenders with personality disorder should adopt the two-dimensional model within the diagnostic formulation. This should include the assessments outlined below.

(a) (i) *Personality disorder* – an assessment involving one or more of the following constructs:

    (1) DSM–IV Axis II categorisation;

    (2) ICD–10 personality disorder categories;

    (3) one of the recognised rating scales, such as the PCL–R (Hare, 1991), the Minnesota Multiphasic Personality Inventory (MMPI; Dahlstrom *et al*, 1975) or the Special Hospital Assessment of Personality and Socialisation (SHAPS) profile; Blackburn, 1992);

    (4) structured clinical interview to provide a psychodynamic formulation.

(ii) *Clinical syndromes* (Axis I) – detailed psychiatric history to cover mental disorders, and including paraphilias and substance misuse. Research instruments should include the lifetime perspective rather than the present mental state alone.

(iii) *Behavioural disorders* – detailed assessment of the patient's behaviour in relation to culturally determined social norms, including social adjustment, work record, quality of interpersonal relationships, criminal behaviour, etc.

(b) *Lifetime perspective* – all three components should be considered from the lifetime perspective according to the present level of functioning and previous patterns of development.

We also recommend an additional assessment:

(c) *Risk assessment.*

By separating these components within the assessment and final diagnostic formulation it becomes easier to observe whether various potential aetiological factors relate primarily to one component or another. Similarly, treatment programmes can then be evaluated according to which component has been individually targeted. For example, medication may not change certain personality traits, but may improve symptoms of major mental disorder or act prophylactically to prevent further episodes, which may in turn have previously interfered with the success of a treatment programme or a patient's ability to cooperate with the treatment programme. Examples of this diagnostic approach using case studies are described by Dolan & Coid (1993).

The basis of an assessment using this two-dimensional construct is the standard psychiatric history, but with specific modifications taking into account the individual's offending behaviour and personality psychopathology. For offender patients, the clinical assessment will concentrate on the forensic context and additional factors such as motivation (see Coid, 1998) and the importance of future risk. There remain, however, several problems with the choice of which construct to use when making the assessment of the personality disorder. Assessment of personality disorder can rarely construct a psychodynamic formulation, a psychological profile based on MMPI scores, and an Axis II categorisation at the same time. As a minimum, Dolan & Coid (1993) have recommended that DSM Axis II categorisation (or ICD–10) together with a PCL–R rating should be carried out in forensic settings for offenders with personality disorder.

The Royal College of Psychiatrists has issued guidance on clinical risk assessment and management for all clinicians in their routine day-to-day practice and we strongly recommend that these same principles are as applicable for offenders with personality disorder. There continue to be further developments in objective risk assessment scales. In an institutional setting, or where there is sufficient time, we recommend the regular use of an instrument such as the Violent Risk Appraisal Guide (VRAG; Harris & Rice, 1984; Rice & Harris, 1995). This is an important scale which was developed from an initial pool of over 40 items through a stepwise discriminant analysis that resulted in the 12 best predictors. The total score on the VRAG displayed a correlation of 0.45 with violent recidivism in a sample of 618 offenders with mental disorders (see also Bonta *et al*, 1998).

Structured clinical assessment interviews for DSM–IV Axis II

Instruments used in research which include the full range of personality disorder categories include:

Structured clinical assessment instruments for DSM–IV Axis II

  (a) SCID–II, Structured Clinical Interview for DSM–IV Personality Disorder (First *et al*, 1995).
  (b) SIDP–IV, Structured Interview for DSM–IV Personality Disorders (Pfohl *et al*, 1995).
  (c) DIPD–IV, Diagnostic Interview for Personality Disorders (Zanarini *et al*, 1994).

Structured clinical assessment instruments for ICD–10

(a) IPDE, International Personality Disorder Examination (Loranger *et al*, 1987, 1994).

(b) SAP, Standardised Assessment of Personality – designed for use with a relative or close friend of a patient (Mann *et al*, 1981).

(c) PAS, Personality Assessment Schedule (Tyrer *et al*, 1979) – a trait-based approach which rejects the standard categorisation of personality disorders in the DSM and ICD–10 classifications, but does provide algorithms for making diagnoses in these systems.

Self-report questionnaires

Self-report questionnaires that make a range of Axis II diagnoses include:

(a) MCMI–III, Millon Clinical Multiaxial Inventory (Millon *et al*, 1997).

(b) PDQ, Personality Disorder Questionnaire (Hyler & Reider, 1984; Hyler, 1994)

(c) SCID–II screen, screening version of the structured clinical interview for DSM–IV.

Self-administered tests cannot substitute for clinical interviews. There is the obvious limitation of their inability to provide the observations, cross-examination and judgement of the experienced clinician. In addition, they are especially prone to false positive diagnoses, resulting in patients receiving an excess of diagnostic labels. They are valuable economically as screening devices, particularly in epidemiological surveys, but cannot be recommended in the routine clinical assessment of offenders with personality disorder.

PCL–R, MMPI and SHAPS

Hare's Psychopathy Checklist (Hare, 1980, 1991) is not a classificatory system but a unidimensional scale of psychopathy consisting of both personality traits and antisocial behaviours. At the heart of this construct is the notion that psychopathy is a unitary syndrome that can be measured using such a scale. During its development, Hare initially took a list of 16 characteristics considered by Cleckley (1976), in his seminal work *The Mask of Sanity,* to be typical of a psychopath and applied them to a series of prisoners (Hare, 1980). A cut-off score of 30 or above out of a maximum of 40 has been used by Hare and colleagues for research purposes to designate subjects as psychopaths.

The instrument has demonstrated high interrater and test–re-test reliability on prisoners and forensic psychiatric hospital in-patients when the checklist is used by properly trained raters (see Hare, 1991).

This instrument has limited usefulness outside of a forensic setting. Nevertheless, it has been shown to predict individuals who fail to cooperate with, or benefit from, certain treatment programmes and who are more likely to re-offend following release from a secure setting.

Although the PCL–R has proved useful in North American populations, there have been few studies of the PCL–R in British or European populations. Those that have been conducted indicate that, although the same constructs are being measured, mean scores are lower, cut-offs to distinguish cases from non-cases may have to be adjusted and some items suffer in cross-cultural translation. The dimensional or categorical nature of the construct of psychopathy as measured by the PCL–R also remains in question (Hare, 1991).

The Special Hospital Assessment of Personality and Socialisation (SHAPS; Blackburn, 1992), which was based on a cluster analysis of the MMPI and items from the Buss–Durkee Hostility and Guilt Inventory (Buss & Durkee, 1957), focuses more specifically on 'psychopathy-related' traits such as impulsivity and hostile interpersonal attitudes, but also contains measures of the 'big five' dimensions, including neurotism and extraversion. This instrument, which includes dimensional scores on several personality dimensions relevant to antisocial behaviour, produces four profiles of offenders (primary psychopath, secondary psychopath, overcontrolled, inhibited). The classification has been replicated in research on murderers, violent offenders and unselected prisoners, suggesting that the typology is robust and represents the main personality types identifiable through self-report measures.

Although there are differences in the pattern of associations of the PCL–R and the SHAPS, reflecting the different personality dimensions they are tapping, the SHAPS offers the advantage of allowing assessment of change on each of its sub-scales, which may be useful in therapeutic evaluation studies.

Recommendations and conclusions

(a) There should be improved teaching of all psychiatric trainees in the assessment of personality disorder. Teaching clinical assessment and the diagnostic formulation of personality disorders should become routine within their teaching programmes.

(b) A standardised approach to the assessment of offenders with personality disorder should now be introduced. We recommend the two-dimensional approach based on the standard psychiatric interview, but consisting of:
  (i)   personality disorder;
  (ii)   clinical syndromes;
  (iii) behavioural disorder; and
  (iv)   lifetime perspective of (i), (ii), (iii).
(c) Risk assessment of offenders with personality disorder should become a routine part of the assessment procedure.
(d) The assessment of offenders with personality disorder should include a categorical classification of personality disorder using DSM–IV (or ICD–10) Axis II. We would also recommend the use of a recognised rating scale.
(e) We do not recommend the use of self-report instruments during clinical assessment for the purpose of making personality disorder diagnoses, although these may have a role in screening.

3   Epidemiology

Executive summary

Epidemiological surveys of the prevalence of personality disorder in the community and in prisons are essential for the development of policy which should not be based on research from highly selected hospital samples. Surveys demonstrate that personality disorder is a highly prevalent form of mental disorder which affects a significant subgroup of the general population and the majority of individuals in prison. This level of morbidity demonstrates that it is entirely beyond the capacity of psychiatric services in hospitals, prisons or the community to deliver treatment to more than a minority. It is now clear that current and future services must be highly selective and focused on specific subgroups of personality-disordered individuals for the delivery of care and treatment to those who are most likely to benefit. It is with this aim that future research should be carried out in the form of epidemiologically-based needs assessment. The most prevalent Axis II disorders among offenders include antisocial, borderline and paranoid personality disorders. However, these conditions remain very difficult to treat and are sometimes intractable (see Chapter 5). Patients selected for admission to secure hospitals are more likely to be female, suffer from borderline personality disorder and have comorbid Axis I or affective symptomatology. Future research must determine whether these are the most appropriate individuals for diversion to the hospital setting.

Planning and development of new facilities for offenders with personality disorder cannot be carried out without an accurate overview of the size of the problem. It is increasingly clear that future needs assessments of these populations must also be carried out within an epidemiological framework (Eastman, 1997). However, there is less information on the prevalence of personality disorders than the major mental disorders, such as schizophrenia. This partly reflects the shorter history of empirical research into the development of diagnostic constructs for personality disorder, but also the fact that few personality disorders, with the exception of antisocial personality disorder, have been routinely included in epidemiological research. There is increasing interest in this field. Recent reviews of the epidemiological literature include Reich & de Girolamo (1997) and, of more relevance to offenders, Moran (1999). There has also been a recent survey of prisoners in England and Wales (Singleton *et al*, 1998) which, for the first time, has included a full range of categories of personality disorder in the penal setting. In addition, there is increasing information on patients with personality disorder who have been treated in secure forensic psychiatry facilities.

True prevalence studies

Since the publication of DSM–III (American Psychiatric Association, 1980) in 1980, there have been several studies, mainly in North America providing data on the prevalence of 'any' personality disorder. Nestadt *et al* (1990, 1991, 1992) detailed the results of a follow-up assessment for personality disorders in the Epidemiologic Catchment Area (ECA) study in a series of reports. They reported a prevalence of 5.9% for a definite diagnosis of personality disorder in different US sites and a prevalence of 9.3% for their combined 'definite' plus 'provisional' diagnostic categories. Casey & Tyrer (1986) found a prevalence of 13% of 'any' personality disorder in a smaller community sample, and Reich *et al* (1989) found 11% using a self-report instrument in a postal survey. Maier *et al* (1992) estimated a prevalence of 10.0% in a sample from Germany.

Table 3.1 summarises the data available on the prevalence of different categories of personality disorder in community surveys.

TABLE 3.1
Personality disorder in community surveys

Personality disorder	%
Antisocial	2.0–3.0
Borderline	1.7–2.0
Narcissistic	0.4
Histrionic	2.1
Paranoid	2.0
Schizoid	0.4–0.9
Schizotypal	0.6–5.6
Avoidant	1.1–1.3
Dependent	1.6–1.7
Compulsive	1.7–2.2
Any	5.9–13.0

From Reich & de Girolamo (1997) and Moran (1999)

Only one category, antisocial personality disorder, has been reliably measured using research diagnostic instruments.

Antisocial personality disorder

When individual categories of personality disorder are examined, there is considerably more information on antisocial personality disorder than any other diagnostic category. This is because antisocial personality disorder has been included as a single Axis II diagnosis in a number of epidemiological studies of major mental disorder. These generally find a prevalence of 2–3% in studies that have been carried out in North America and other developed countries (Bland, 1988; Wells *et al*, 1989; Zimmerman & Coryell, 1989; Nestadt *et al*, 1990; Robins *et al*, 1991). Unfortunately, there are no data on the prevalence of antisocial personality disorders in the general population in the UK.

These studies have found antisocial personality disorder to be more frequent among males than females, among younger adults, those living in urban areas and in inner-city areas compared to suburban areas of cities, and among the lower socio-economic classes. Research has confirmed that the diagnosis is associated with high use of medical services.

Borderline personality disorder

Borderline personality disorder is the most common personality disorder seen in most psychiatric settings and is over-represented in clinical populations because of the tendency towards help-seeking. In their review of the literature, de Girolamo & Reich (1993) concluded that the highest rates are found in the 19–34 year age range, with rates declining with age. As well as being high users of mental health services, people with borderline personality disorder frequently have poor marital relationships, higher rates of physical disability, job difficulties, alcohol misuse, and psychosexual problems. Several authors have also found higher percentages among females, particularly in clinical samples, and much higher percentages in Whites than Blacks. However, it remains unclear whether there is truly a gender difference and more research is required on ethnic subgroups.

Other personality disorder categories

Table 3.2 demonstrates the prevalences of other categories of personality disorder from a limited number of community surveys or studies which included community controls.

Treated prevalence

The growing evidence that personality disorders present a considerable burden of care upon mental health services makes it essential to study their prevalence in these settings and then compare this with true prevalences in the community. It is well known that there are problems when using treated rates for drawing any inference about the true prevalence of personality disorders or the need for service provision. For example, there is likely to be bias in findings in these settings due to: (a) differences in the availability of treatment; (b) the role of cultural factors in help-seeking behaviour; (c) differences in the severity of different disorders; (d) the potential influence of other comorbid psychiatric disorders; and (e) differences among the personality disorders in the likelihood of seeking treatment. During the mid-1980s, 7.6% of all psychiatric admissions to hospitals in England and Wales had a diagnosis of personality disorder using the ICD classification (Department of Health and Social Security, 1985). This is likely to have been a considerable underestimate as any non-personality disorder psychiatric condition would usually have been recorded in preference to a co-occurring personality disorder. This problem is also reflected in a study by Oldham & Skodol (1991), who

TABLE 3.2
Prevalence of personality disorder using SCID–II[1]
clinical interviews by prisoner type (n=496)

Personality disorder	Male remand (n=181) %	Male sentenced (n=120) %	Female (n=105) %
Antisocial	63	49	31
Paranoid	29	20	16
Borderline	23	14	20
Avoidant	14	7	11
Obsessive–compulsive	7	11	11
Narcissistic	8	7	6
Schizoid	8	6	4
Dependent	4	1	5
Schizotypal	2	2	4
Histrionic	1	2	4
Cluster A	35	25	19
Cluster B	62	48	40
Cluster C	21	15	22
Any	78	64	50

1. SCID–II, Stuctured Clinical Interview for DSM–III–R Personality disorders (First *et al*, 1995).

investigated the prevalence of personality disorders among the 129 268 patients treated in New York State mental health facilities in 1988. Using the centralised database system, they found that 10.8% received a personality disorder diagnosis. However, personality disorder was the primary diagnosis for only 1.2% of patients. When diagnoses were made by clinicians, only 0.2% received more than one personality disorder diagnosis.

Reich & de Girolamo (1997) have summarised findings from a large number of in-patient and out-patient psychiatric samples. Although there are multiple problems due to differences in sampling, diagnostic criteria, assessment methods, availability of mental health services, prevalence of Axis I disorders and socio-cultural factors, the authors did find certain consistencies across studies. The most prevalent personality disorder in treated samples appears to be borderline, both in in-patient and out-patient settings, followed by schizotypal and histrionic. These three disorders appear to be characterised by low social functioning. They were especially common in in-patient settings as their symptomatology often had resulted in hospitalisation because of suicidal behaviour, substance misuse and cognitive perceptual abnormality. In out-patient settings, dependent and passive–aggressive personality disorders were also common.

Prison populations

Although there have been several surveys of personality disorder in prison populations, there remains a series of problems when attempting to obtain an accurate prevalence of personality disorders among prisoners, in particular the methodological problem of sampling. Most surveys have been carried out in single institutions, often in penitentiaries or prisons that have a concentration of professional and hardened criminals, and where there is likely to be a disproportionate number of subjects found to have antisocial personality disorder or high scores on the Psychopathy Checklist (Revised) (PCL–R; Hare, 1991). Also, research diagnostic instruments have rarely been used, except in the case of the Diagnostic Interview Schedule, and then only for the single category of antisocial personality disorder. However, the recent survey of psychiatric morbidity among prisoners in England and Wales does provide a representative picture of a full range of Axis II disorders in a national survey (Singleton *et al*, 1998).

Previous studies in North America have found between 39 and 61.5% of subjects with antisocial personality disorder using DSM–III diagnoses. These were restricted to penitentiary populations where a higher proportion of individuals with this diagnosis were likely to be concentrated (Hare, 1983; Bland *et al*, 1990; Cote & Hodgins, 1990). Jordan *et al* (1996) found that 11.9% of female prisoners had antisocial personality disorders in a similar institutional survey and Teplin *et al* (1996) also found a lifetime prevalence of antisocial personality disorder of 13.8% in a female remand population in the USA. In contrast, Cooke (1994) found that only 3% of male prisoners in the Scottish survey were psychopaths using a cut-off score of 30 and above on the PCL–R.

The most extensive previous survey of UK prisoners found that 10% of sentenced males had personality disorder. In a later study of remanded prisoners 11.2% of males, 15.5% of females and 11.7% of male youths had personality disorder (Maden *et al*, 1993). However, neither survey employed research diagnostic interviews. The diagnosis of personality disorder was made instead by clinicians using their clinical judgement following an interview that was primarily designed to elicit Axis I clinical syndromes.

More recently, a two-stage survey was carried out in all prisons in England and Wales by the Office of National Statistics (Singleton *et al*, 1998). A sample of over 3000 prisoners was interviewed by lay interviewers who administered a screening version of the SCID–II interview. A one in six sub-sample was then randomly selected for re-interview by trained clinicians using the Structured Clinical Interview for DSM–IV Axis II disorders. Table 3.2 shows the prevalence of personality disorder by prisoner type. Antisocial personality disorder demonstrated the highest prevalence of any category: 63% of male remand prisoners, 49% of sentenced prisoners and 31% of female prisoners. Paranoid personality disorder was the second most prevalent condition: 29% of male remand prisoners, 20% of male sentenced prisoners and 16% of female prisoners. Borderline personality disorder was more common than paranoid personality disorder in female prisoners.

Table 3.3 demonstrates the prevalence of psychopathy according to prisoner type, using the PCL–R, and shows a somewhat higher prevalence than that found by Cooke (1994) in Scotland. However, much lower prevalences were found than in the North American penitentiary populations studied by Hare (1991).

When examining the findings from the SCID–II screening question-naires which had been administered to the larger sample of over 3000 prisoners interviewed by lay interviewers, it was found that in the male remand group individuals with personality disorder were more likely to be in the youngest age group of 16–20 years, to be White and held following offences of burglary, robbery or theft. They were less likely to be married or held for a drug offence. Subjects with personality disorder were also more likely than other prisoners to have been held in solitary confinement or to have received punishments in prison resulting in their being given extended sentences. A relationship was also found between personality disorder and a perceived lack of social support in the community from relatives, friends or acquaintances and other prisoners. Subjects who reported living off crime before imprisonment were most likely to have a diagnosis of personality disorder. Personality-disordered individuals had the highest prevalence of stressful life events over their lifetime in the survey.

Being born in the UK appeared to be significantly associated with having evidence of personality disorder. Once country of birth had been taken into account, people who classified themselves in the Black or 'Other' ethnic groups were then more likely to have a diagnosis of personality disorder than those in the White group.

Prevalence of personality disorder in secure forensic psychiatry facilities

Although there is increasing information on personality disorder among patients detained in secure forensic psychiatry facilities, few studies have used research diagnostic instruments. Table 3.4 demonstrates the findings from a survey of female patients detained under the Mental Health Act 1983 legal category of psychopathic disorder in three Special Hospitals from 1984 to 1987 and male patients detained under the same legal category in Broadmoor Hospital from 1984 to 1986, which used the SCID–II (Coid, 1992). The table is useful for comparison with the findings of the national survey of prisoners in England and Wales in Tables 3.2 and 3.3.

TABLE 3.3
Prevalence of psychopathy according to prisoner type using the Psychopathy Checklist – Revised (n=497). (Further information available from Professor Coid upon request.)

PCL–R scores	Male remand (n=181) %	Male sentenced (n=211) %	Female (n=105) %
Less than 25	77	86	93
25–29	14	8	5
25 and above	23	14	7
30 and above[1]	9	6	2

1. Subjects scoring 30 and above designated as having a psychopathic disorder

TABLE 3.4
*Personality disorder in special hospital surveys
using SCID–II for DSM–III (from Coid, 1992)*

	Females with psychopathic disorder[1] (*n*=93) (%)	Males with psychopathic disorder[1] (*n*=86) (%)
Borderline	91	55
Antisocial	44	38
Narcissistic	37	45
Paranoid	46	28
Passive–aggressive	28	16
Schizotypal	25	19
Histrionic	19	13
Avoidant	36	8
Dependent	25	20
Schizoid	11	13
Compulsive	11	14
Masochistic	9	4
'Psychopath' (PCL–R)	31	23

1. Refers to Mental Health Act 1983 legal category of psychopathic disorder

Legally detained individuals with a psychopathic disorder contrast with prisoners in that in both males and females borderline personality was the most prevalent of all Axis II disorders, compared to antisocial personality disorder in prisoners. There was a higher prevalence of narcissistic personality disorder and conditions such as schizotypal and histrionic personality disorders which had a low prevalence in the prison sample.

The male : female ratio of individuals who had a psychopathic disorder also appeared to be reversed in the secure hospital samples. More female patients scored above the cut-off, which designated them as having a psychopathic disorder using the PCL–R (Hare, 1980), in contrast to the prison survey. The overall prevalence of psychopathy using Hare's scale was considerably higher in both males and females detained under the legal category of psychopathic disorder in the high security hospital study than in the prison survey.

These findings suggest that patients compulsorily detained under the legal category of psychopathic disorder are highly selected and may be an unusual subgroup of offenders with personality disorder. The importance of selection is further emphasised in the study by Coid (1992), which made a further comparison with an additional sample of prisoners who had been placed in special units for those who had been highly disruptive or dangerous. A significant subgroup of these men had been rejected for admission to a high security hospital. The prevalence of psychopathy in this group measured using Hare's scale was 77%. The importance of selectivity is further emphasised by the fact that only one male subject in the hospital sample (Table 3.4) was of African–Caribbean ethnic origin.

Personality disorder in secure forensic psychiatry facilities

An unpublished study (details available from Professor Coid upon request) has examined all admissions of patients with a primary diagnosis of personality disorder to both high and medium secure facilities from a geographically representative area covering over half of England during a seven-year study period, 1988–1994. There were a total of 3910 admissions during the seven-year period and 84% of these involved patients with mental illness, 16% with personality disorder. The proportion of personality-disordered admissions to high security (28%) facilities was significantly higher than admissions to medium security (13%) facilities. Overall, there were significantly more females among the personality-disordered subgroup (32%) compared with the mentally ill (12%). Patients with personality disorders also tended to be younger on admission and were more likely to be White. The findings confirmed previous observations that very few individuals with personality disorder admitted to secure psychiatric facilities are of African–Caribbean origin (6% in this study, in contrast to 24% of the mentally ill).

Patients with personality disorder were more likely to be referred by their lawyer, the Home Office or the Probation Service for admission. Admissions to medium security facilities were likely to be referred for rehabilitation by psychiatrists at high security hospitals. A larger proportion of patients with a mental illness were admitted to forensic psychiatry facilities following difficult or dangerous non-criminal behaviour in a local psychiatric hospital compared with patients with personality disorder, the majority of whom were admitted following criminal behaviour. There were few overall differences in the categories of offending behaviour that had led to admissions, but patients with personality disorder were admitted more frequently following serious sexual offences and offences of arson. However, when previous histories of criminality were examined, patients with personality disorder had more previous convictions for sex offending, arson, criminal damage and acquisitive offences such as burglary, theft, fraud and alcohol-related offences. They were also more likely to have been in borstals or young offenders institutions previously and to have served previous sentences of imprisonment.

The majority of patients were diagnosed as suffering from DSM–III–R (American Psychiatric Association, 1987) Cluster B antisocial and borderline personality disorders, followed by dependent and paranoid personality disorders. However, these diagnoses were based on case note reviews. Although carried out by a clinically trained researcher, it is likely that additional diagnoses would have emerged had these subjects been interviewed. Patients with borderline personality disorder were more likely to be female and younger than other subjects. Individuals with antisocial, paranoid, schizoid and dependent personality disorders were significantly more likely to be male.

A comparison was also made between patients with personality disorder who were admitted to high security and medium secure facilities. Those admitted to high security were more likely to be referred from prison following a criminal charge or conviction and were more likely to be detained on admission under the Mental Health Act category of psychopathic disorder. Homicide and serious offences of rape and buggery were significantly more frequent in the high security admissions. In contrast, significantly more admissions to medium security facilities came from other (non-secure) psychiatric facilities in the community. The patients with personality disorder admitted into high security facilities were also more likely to have previous convictions for violence, major sex offences, acquisitive offences and to have served previous sentences in prisons and young offenders institutions. They were also more likely to have a diagnosis of antisocial personality disorder compared with those admitted to medium security facilities.

These findings confirm that secure forensic psychiatry services in England prioritise the severely mentally ill. English forensic psychiatrists are also highly selective when admitting patients with personality disorder, who are by no means representative of offenders with personality disorder in prison or the community. In general, personality-disordered hospital admissions are more likely to be female, White, and admitted following sexual offences and offences of arson compared with the mentally ill. When treatment or admission of a patient with personality disorder is offered by a forensic psychiatrist, the admission is also more likely to be to high security. However, an important finding (further details available from Professor Coid upon request) was that 70% of both the personality disordered and mentally ill had previously been admitted to a psychiatric hospital, and that a third of both had previously been compulsorily admitted following a criminal offence. This would suggest that the personality-disordered subgroup was already well known to psychiatric services.

It is probable that this had produced a major effect on the selection procedure for admission, with forensic psychiatrists selecting those individuals with personality disorder who had previously been treated elsewhere. Whether the subgroup represented patients who had previously responded to treatment and exhibited less serious behavioural disturbance in hospital, indicating that they were more manageable, or whether they presented with symptoms of comorbid mental illness or specific traits of personality disorder which appeared more likely to respond to treatment, could not be identified from this study.

The presence of lifetime Axis I comorbidity could also have been a key factor in influencing selection for treatment. It was observed that many subjects had comorbid clinical syndromes despite a primary diagnosis of personality disorder. Female patients with borderline personality disorder admitted to high security hospitals have previously been observed to present with severe mood swings (Coid, 1993*b*). Axis I comorbidity and the presence of symptoms usually associated with mental illness but associated in these offenders with specific categories of personality disorder (mainly borderline personality disorder) may have had a profound influence on the decision to admit to a secure hospital setting. It remains unclear, however, why relatively few admissions to hospital of offender patients with personality disorder are from ethnic minorities. As prison surveys indicate that a substantial number present with these conditions, the possibility remains that there may be a tendency to exclude individuals with personality disorder from ethnic minorities as unsuitable for treatment in secure hospitals. This question would require further research to clarify precisely the processes that are taking place to account for these findings.

Recommendations and conclusions

(a) Personality disorder is highly prevalent in the general population and can be diagnosed in the majority of prisoners. Only a proportion is likely to respond to therapeutic interventions and the current capacity of psychiatric services to intervene is severely limited.

(b) Future research should be directed at the identification of those individuals who are most likely to respond to therapeutic interventions. This would avoid scarce resources being dissipated without any benefits in outcome.

(c) Offenders with personality disorder detained in secure hospitals represent an unusual and highly selected subgroup. A disproportionate number are female. Further research is required into this selection process and whether it is appropriate in terms of treatment outcome and cost-effectiveness.

(d) Epidemiological surveys would be useful in identifying the prevalence of personality-disordered individuals in different populations who are at high risk of offending in the future.

4 Longitudinal development

Executive summary

Longitudinal studies of conduct disorder and delinquency are of major importance in formulating future policies for preventing the development of adverse adult outcomes such as personality disorder and criminality. The majority of children with conduct disorders do not develop antisocial personality disorders. However, a significant subgroup still have multiple problems in adulthood. Future research should aim to identify more accurately those factors which predict severe adverse outcomes with a view to targeting children who are at greatest risk. Further studies are required in the UK into risk and protective factors. These may have considerable importance in the refinement of preventive interventions that have been tested elsewhere (see Chapter 5). It is possible that new longitudinal studies may ultimately suggest new interventions for both primary prevention in childhood and adult offenders with personality disorder. The findings from previous research are not encouraging for those with antisocial personality disorder or where persistent and pervasive criminality is a dominant feature. By adulthood the behaviour of most subjects appears recalcitrant and unamenable to therapeutic interventions.

A longitudinal perspective on disordered behaviour and personality disorder is vital. The diagnostic categories of personality disorder in the DSM–IV (American Psychiatric Association, 1994) and ICD–10 (World Health Organization, 1992) classifications represent a series of clinical hypotheses, most of which are longitudinal in nature. These disorders are considered to begin in adolescence or earlier, persist for many years and adversely affect long-term functioning. They are also seen to influence the presentation, course and response to treatment of the Axis I clinical syndromes. With the exception of antisocial personality disorder, there is a dearth of empirical research regarding the longitudinal course of the personality disorders.

There are many problems in carrying out longitudinal research in this area. First, our current constructs of disordered personality, and the related instruments for assessment, are continuing to evolve so that stable case identification remains difficult. Second, although the clinical samples included in most longitudinal studies are clearly impaired and are, by definition, presenting for treatment, they are subject to a variety of selection biases. Their course may also be affected by treatment. The psychosocial impairments of personality disorder among individuals in the community are not well documented either. It is likely that most do not seek psychiatric treatment, yet are still dysfunctional. There is also the problem that individuals with personality disorders tend to be less compliant and less stable residentially and are therefore more difficult to follow-up longitudinally than other subjects.

There are many important questions that need to be addressed, particularly with a view to treatment and management – these will have important bearings on the recommendations of this report. For example, what are the childhood antecedents of these disorders and what are the natural courses of these conditions? Furthermore, we need to know how life experiences and treatment may affect the course of these conditions. Unfortunately, the only available body of information on longitudinal development which is of sufficient quality to provide any useful conclusions for new directions in the treatment and management of offenders with personality disorder is for the categories antisocial and borderline (and to a lesser extent schizotypal) personality disorder. Nevertheless, we have observed in Chapter 3 that the most prevalent conditions are in fact antisocial and borderline personality disorder, the latter being particularly prevalent among female offenders.

Conduct disorder

Several long-term prospective studies of delinquency and behavioural disorder in children have attempted to discover whether behaviour and associated personality traits have long-term stability and to identify early predictors of adverse outcomes. There are, however, problems with the long-term study of antisocial personality traits as these may be expressed differently at different ages. Moreover, continuity of deviant behaviour does not necessarily reflect continuity of underlying causative personality abnormality, as the meaning and motivators of behavioural features may vary with age. Research has confirmed that a significant proportion of children who demonstrate conduct disorders in childhood show poor peer relationships, come from disadvantaged, disordered and disorganised family environments, and have parents who suffer from mental illness (especially personality disorder), display criminality and practise violent or erratic child-rearing. Children with conduct disorders are more likely to exhibit an adverse outcome in adulthood, including crime, low occupational achievement, substance misuse and marital instability. In most cases the original childhood behavioural problems must be present for the adverse outcome, although a subgroup does not display signs until middle or late adolescence.

Markedly different longitudinal courses can be observed. For example, a small subgroup of individuals with a relatively normal childhood can still have an adverse adult outcome. It appears that overall recovery from behavioural problems presenting before adulthood is common in the majority of children, a subgroup of even the most difficult becoming normal adults. However, a further subgroup remains who not only demonstrate conduct disorder and problems of adult adjustment, but also have persisting antisocial behaviour into the fourth decade.

It has been estimated that between 4% and 10% of children in Britain and the USA meet the criteria for conduct disorder (Rutter *et al*, 1975; Kazdin, 1987; Institute of Medicine, 1989). Estimates have also indicated that conduct disorder is present in one-third to half of all children and adolescent clinic referrals (Robins, 1981; Herbert, 1987). This condition is characterised by a persistent pattern of behaviour in which the child violates the basic rights of others and the major age-appropriate social norms. Up to 40% of children so diagnosed can be expected to have a range of serious psychosocial disturbances in adulthood (Robins, 1970; Rutter & Giller, 1983).

Conduct disorder is one of the three sub-classes of disruptive behavioural disorder of children, along with attention-deficit hyper-activity disorder and oppositional defiant disorder. Clinical evidence suggests that these disorders may transform from one to the other, but usually in a particular order from attention-deficit hyperactivity disorder to oppositional defiant disorder, to conduct disorder and ultimately to antisocial personality disorder in adulthood. It is unclear whether these conditions should be considered as entirely separate or whether conduct disorder might be better conceptualised as the middle phase of a very chronic psychiatric disorder beginning in early life and continuing into early adulthood, but which can still abort at any point along the way and show improvement (Loeber *et al*, 1991).

From its appearance in early childhood, aggressiveness is the most stable personality characteristic of conduct disorder (Loeber, 1982), although the aggression will be expressed differently at different stages of development. For example, Aschenbach & Edelbrock (1981) found that mothers reported younger problem-children to be argumentative, stubborn and prone to tantrums while older children demonstrated oppositional behaviours. At a later date, they present with fire-setting and stealing and finally truancy, vandalism and substance misuse. It is of considerable importance that Loeber (1982) has identified from a review of the literature four factors which predict of chronic delinquency following conduct disorder in childhood:

(a) frequency of antisocial behaviours;
(b) variety of antisocial behaviours;
(c) age of onset; and
(d) the presence of antisocial behaviour in more than one setting.

These factors not only predispose to adult antisocial personality disorder (Robins *et al*, 1991), but also to substance misuse (Hesslebrock, 1986), major mental disorder in a subgroup (Robins & Price, 1991) and a higher rate of violent death (Rydelius, 1988).

Follow-up studies of conduct disorder

A detailed review of follow-up studies is beyond the scope of this report and we have been selective in describing those which illustrate the main factors that should be considered in this area. In what is perhaps the most famous longitudinal study, Robins (1966) followed-up a series of children referred to a child guidance clinic for antisocial behaviour and traced them 30 years later, comparing them with children referred for other reasons (primarily with neurotic symptoms) and control subjects from local schools in the neighbourhood of the clinic. The original sample of children with conduct disorder had parents of low occupational status and only a third were with both parents at the time of referral. A third had spent at least six months in an institution or foster home and many of their fathers had deserted the families and/or drank heavily. Many mothers failed to keep house or supervise their children. A substantial proportion had siblings with behavioural disorder and most were behind at school when referred, with 52% of boys and 30% of girls officially classified as juvenile delinquents. At 30-year follow-up the children with antisocial disorders were more likely to have left the area of origin and three-quarters of the men and 40% of the women had been arrested for non-traffic offences, almost half of the males for at least one major crime. Arrests for serious offences such as rape and murder in adulthood were found only in the children with conduct disorders. Prostitution was found only in the histories of females with conduct disorder. Divorce and repetitive remarriage were more common in those with conduct disorders and Robins observed that the women tended to choose husbands who were unfaithful, deserted or failed to support them. There was a high rate of childlessness in this group, but those who did have children were more likely to have behavioural problems than the two control groups. More than 20% of mothers with antisocial behaviour in childhood had had a child who had been arrested by the time of follow-up. Occupational history in adulthood was characterised by lower social status and more frequent unemployment.

Remission and improvement in adulthood could be assessed in the majority of these children and Robins judged that 12% were in remission 30 years later (subjects were then in their fourth or fifth decade); 27% showed a greatly reduced range in severity of antisocial behaviour but 60% still showed little improvement. The improvement observed in the first two subgroups appeared to occur progressively in each decade, most often in the 30–40 year age range. It was thought that special life circumstances, sometimes the threat of further punishments following arrest, were a decisive factor. However, Robins believed that neither hospitalisation nor the experience of psychotherapy during the lives of her subjects with sociopathic disorders had any positive association with improvement.

Robins (1978) later replicated her original study with additional cohorts growing up in different eras and living in different parts of the USA. She argued that her findings indicated that adult and childhood antisocial behaviours both form individual syndromes and that these two syndromes are closely connected. She also concluded that manifestation of adult antisocial behaviour as a pervasive syndrome virtually required a preceding pattern of childhood antisocial behaviour. It was on the basis of these empirical observations that the diagnostic construct of antisocial personality disorder was subsequently developed in the DSM classification system. However, the majority of children with conduct disorder did not go on to become adults with antisocial personality disorder. It appeared to Robins that the variety of antisocial behaviour in childhood was in itself a better predictor of antisocial behaviour than any particular individual form. Furthermore, behaviour in childhood was also a better predictor of the future than family background or social class.

Longitudinal studies of delinquency

In a series of studies of the development of delinquency, West & Farrington systematically surveyed a sample of boys when aged eight years recruited from a working-class neighbourhood in London (West, 1969, 1982; West & Farrington, 1973, 1977). By the age of 25, one-third had acquired a criminal record. Different patterns of criminal career were observed within the convicted group and the authors roughly classified their convicted subjects into four subgroups: juvenile one-time offenders, latecomers to crime, temporary recidivists and persisting delinquents. The persisting delinquents tended to start their criminal careers at a particularly early age, to sustain frequent convictions as juveniles and to continue to acquire convictions into their twenties. They were generally from the worst, most deprived family backgrounds. They stood out as the most conspicuously deviant group, both during school years and in early adulthood. This subgroup appeared to overlap with the antisocial subjects identified by Robins in her studies. By their early twenties, the recidivist subjects were more likely to have been unemployed, spent more money on alcohol and tobacco per week, were living in home conditions which were poor, have unpaid debts, were more likely to be cohabiting rather than married and were more likely to be separated from their children by forming other relationships. Within sexual relationships they were less likely to use contraceptives and more had been involved in fighting and admitted to be still involved in criminality.

The researchers attempted to examine features which might change the course of the delinquency careers and identified four factors which appeared to influence the life course.

(a) Going to the wrong school – there were somewhat more delinquents than expected from schools that had overall high delinquency rates.
(b) Getting married – marriage sometimes appeared to have a restraining effect upon delinquents in the study.
(c) Getting caught – an increasingly deviant attitude and behaviour was observed following first conviction.
(d) Moving away – moving away from inner London appeared to have a beneficial effect upon continuing crime.

Career criminals

Research has shown that a small segment of the population is responsible for a large proportion of serious crime. Wolfgang *et al* (1972) reported that in a series of all males born in Philadelphia, USA still living there 10–18 years later, approximately 6–8% were responsible for 51% of offences by the cohort as a whole. Similar findings have emerged for imprisoned and convicted samples (Petersilia *et al*, 1978; Peterson & Braiker, 1980). Similarly, a study of individuals incarcerated for robbery in the USA indicated that their average rate of offending was five robberies per year, but that 5% of the sample had committed 180–400 robberies each (Blumstein & Cohen, 1979). Another study of 24 000 middle-aged US prisoners found that 14% had been continuously involved in crime since adolescence (Langan & Greenfield, 1983).

Delinquent careers can develop along several trajectories (Smith, 1984). However, for career criminals, persistence through four successive stages can be observed (Walters, 1990).

(a) Pre-criminal, 0–18 years.
(b) Early criminal, 18–mid-20s.
(c) Advanced, late 20s–early 40s.
(d) Criminal burn-outs/maturity from the early 40s.

Pre-criminal behaviour is rarely specialised but larceny, burglary and car theft are the most common offences (LeBlanc & Frechette, 1989). These offences are frequently committed in the company of other adolescents, and thrill-seeking is an important motivator. This stage appears to hold the greatest prospect for change and a significant proportion of juveniles do not continue their criminality on into adulthood. During the second stage, the number of individuals committing offences steadily declines (Blumstein & Cohen, 1987), but a subgroup moves towards career criminality as they find themselves in contact with new criminal associates (often met during incarceration), learn new criminal techniques and gain status in the criminal subculture. The overall number of crimes may decrease but their seriousness and the value of property stolen will increase, as do violent offences (West & Farrington, 1977; Petersilia *et al*, 1978).

Voluntary drop-out from crime is at its lowest during this advanced criminal stage. Walters (1990) described these individuals as now having committed themselves to a criminal lifestyle with an associated cognitive style. In the early 40s, a further stage is reached which Hirschi & Gottfredson (1983) describe as corresponding to the mid-life transition where some individuals will begin to demonstrate maturity – a change in their thinking, values and motivation – and terminate their criminal behaviour. For others who remain on the fringes of crime, this period is described as 'burn-out' because of an accompanying decline in physical and mental energy. However, a smaller subgroup fails to re-evaluate their lives and continues to engage in significant criminal behaviour.

Risk and protective factors

Rutter (1989) has emphasised the need to research both risk and protective factors leading to a poor outcome in adulthood. Risk factors are those that influence the probability of a child developing an emotional or behavioural disorder or other form of adverse adult outcome. Protective factors refer to those that protect them from an environment or constitution that places them at high risk of developing such an outcome (Rutter, 1985).

Hechtman (1991) has suggested grouping these factors in the following ways.

Characteristics relating to the child

Children with health problems, including problems during pregnancy, perinatally or during infancy, are more at risk of adult disorder (Werner & Smith, 1982). Children with difficult temperaments are also less adaptive, particularly to new environments or environmental stress, and may be less socially and emotionally responsive to others. They may also have a less reflective cognitive style and be more impulsive, with difficulty controlling their impulses and their aggression. This will in turn interact with their social environment where they are less able to elicit positive responses from their carers and thus find solace and satisfaction (Rutter 1979; Anthony, 1987; Cohler, 1987). Although intelligence is not traditionally considered important in the development of personality disorder and offending behaviour, many studies attest to the superior adult achievement of children with a higher IQ. However, such a constitutional advantage will directly interact with other factors of personality environment so that low IQ can show a complex relationship to delinquency (West, 1982). Resilient children also appear to have a greater sense of autonomy and more positive self-esteem, better empathy, social skills and an ability to relate to peers. They are more able to ask for help from others and are generally more optimistic about themselves and their future.

Family factors

Low socio-economic status clearly relates to the ability of parents to confer various opportunities on their children. Adverse outcome is not related directly to low status without additional mediating factors such as parental competence, living in a delinquent neighbourhood, etc. Authors have frequently stressed the importance of a warm, cohesive, and supportive family environment in influencing outcome (Rutter, 1979; Werner & Smith, 1982; Garmezy, 1985; Anthony, 1987). Adverse factors include psychiatric disorder in parents (especially personality disorder), marital discord, loss of parent (especially due to divorce), one parent family situations, large family size (especially with little space between successive children), institutional care of the child, inconsistent discipline, violence between parents, criminality in parents and lack of structured care in the family environment (Kellam *et al*, 1977; Oliver & Buchanan, 1979; Offord, 1982; West, 1982; Beardslee *et al*, 1983; Rutter & Giller, 1983; Rutter & Quinton, 1984; Quinton & Rutter, 1984; Garmezy, 1985; Oliver, 1988; Lewis *et al*, 1989; Rae-Grant *et al*, 1989).

Larger social and physical environments

Members of the extended family, friends, schools and religious organisations can provide important protective support for children at risk. Change in circumstances over the lifespan, including moving away from the high crime area where drugs are freely available or from delinquent associates and later forming a stable relationship with a partner, can all positively influence outcome (Werner & Smith, 1982; West, 1982; Robins & McEvoy, 1990).

A series of surveys by Werner and colleagues involving a multi-racial cohort of children born on the Hawaiian island of Kauai have provided an important source of data on longitudinal development and the interaction of social and biological factors influencing outcome in adulthood (Werner *et al*, 1971; Werner & Smith, 1977, 1982; Werner, 1985). The main measures of adverse outcome included either a history of arrest or a psychiatric history by the age of 18 years. Box 4.1 lists the vulnerability and stress factors that were observed to relate to an adverse adult outcome in this study and Box 4.2 lists the protective factors relating to a positive outcome. Werner and colleagues observed that protective factors could lead to a good outcome even in the presence of major risk factors in infancy and sources of stress during childhood and adolescence. Thus, despite an upbringing in poor conditions, and with a higher than average rate of perinatal stress, low birth weight, etc., certain children who otherwise developed normally appeared good natured and affectionate in their early years, were able to focus attention and control their impulses, and thereby developed into normal adulthood. Werner proposed a transactional model of development, noting that in a situation of disadvantage through an accumulative number of stressful life events, more protective factors in the children or in their care-giving environment were needed to counterbalance these negative aspects and to ensure a positive developmental outcome. Optimal adaptive development appeared to be characterised by a balance between the power of the person and the power of the social and physical environment. A therapeutic intervention on behalf of children might be conceptualised as an attempt to restore this balance, either by decreasing a young person's exposure to risk or stressful life

---

Box 4.1 Vulnerability and stress factors relating to adverse adult outcome in the Kauai Longitudinal Study

Major risk factors at birth:
(a) chronic poverty;
(b) mother having little education;
(c) moderate to severe perinatal complications;
(d) developmental delays or irregularities;
(e) genetic abnormalities;
(f) parental psychopathology.

Major sources of stress during childhood and adolescence:
(a) prolonged separation from primary care-giver in first year;
(b) birth of younger sibling within two years;
(c) serious repeated childhood illnesses;
(d) parental physical illness;
(e) parental mental illness;
(f) sibling with disability, learning or behaviour problem;
(g) chronic family discord;
(h) father's absence;
(i) loss of job, sporadic employment of parents;
(j) change of residence;
(k) change of school;
(l) divorce of parents;
(m) remarriage and entrance of step-parent into household;
(n) departure or death of close friend or older sibling;
(o) foster home placement;
(p) teenage pregnancy (females).

---

events, or by increasing the number of protective factors (competency, sources of support) that the individual can draw upon within him- or herself or his or her care-giving environment. Some of these factors will be identified within Chapter 5 which deals with the primary prevention of the development of antisocial personality disorder.

Borderline personality disorder

Earlier follow-up studies of patients with borderline personality disorder in the 1970s were of brief duration and used broad and

---

Box 4.2 Protective factors relating to positive adult outcome in the
Kauai Longitudinal Study

Within the child:
(a) integrity of the central nervous system;
(b) birth order (first);
(c) high activity level;
(d) good natured, affectionate disposition;
(e) responsive to people;
(f) free of distressing habits;
(g) positive social orientation;
(h) autonomy;
(i) advanced self-help skills;
(j) age-appropriate sensory–motor and perceptual skills;
(k) adequate communication skills;
(l) ability to focus attention and control impulses;
(m) special interests and hobbies;
(n) positive self-concept;
(o) internal locus of control;
(p) desire to improve self.

Within the care-giving environment:
(a) four or fewer children spaced more than two years apart;
(b) much attention paid to infant during first year;
(c) positive parent–child relationship in early childhood;
(d) additional care-givers besides mother;
(e) care by siblings and grandparents;
(f) mother has some steady employment outside household;
(g) availability of kin and neighbours for emotional support;
(h) structure and rules in household;
(i) shared values – a sense of coherence;
(j) close peer friends;
(k) availability of counsel by teachers and/or ministers;
(l) access to special services (health, education, social services).

---

unsystematic diagnostic criteria. During the 1980s, studies included larger numbers over longer intervals and utilised the DSM classification or closely related criteria (Kroll *et al*, 1985; Plakun *et al*, 1985; McGlashan, 1986; Paris *et al*, 1987; Stone, 1990). These studies followed patients with borderline personality disorder who were admitted to ordinary psychiatric hospitals in North America in the 1960s and 1970s and traced them at intervals over 10–30 years. The outcome was generally favourable, with two-thirds in each study clinically improved at follow-up, although many had residual mild symptoms. Patients with borderline personality disorder were less likely to be married and to have children, but a subgroup demonstrated a dramatic improvement and were later successful professionally. However, approximately one-third of patients with borderline personality disorder had a poor outcome and could be divided into two categories, those who committed suicide and those who were chronically impaired. Two studies demonstrated very similar suicide rates of 8% (Paris *et al*, 1988) and 9% (Stone, 1990), although an additional proportion who survived were known to have made serious suicidal attempts. Poor outcome was associated with alcohol misuse, chaotic impulsivity and a history of parental brutality or sexual molestation. The risk of suicide was greatly increased when comorbid alcohol misuse and depression were combined with borderline personality disorder.

Those within the chronically impaired group were observed to be persistently hostile, could not sustain close relationships and did not cooperate with treatment, frequently signing themselves out of hospital against advice. A number of these individuals also developed more serious affective illnesses, including bipolar affective disorders, but evolution into schizophrenia was rare. The presence of antisocial traits was important in predicting chronic impairment. Comorbid antisocial personality disorder also appeared to increase the risk of suicide. However, the number of subjects with antisocial personality disorder in these longitudinal studies of patients admitted to general psychiatric hospitals was small. Further longitudinal research is needed with people with borderline personality disorder who offend in view of the evidence that comorbid antisocial personality disorder and/or a long history of impulsivity and hostility constitutes a subgroup of individuals with borderline personality disorder with particularly poor prognoses. These individuals are more likely to be found in prisons and secure hospital settings rather than in ordinary psychiatric hospitals.

Recommendations and conclusions

(a) Further longitudinal research is required in the UK to identify the major risk and protective factors. This could facilitate the development of new therapeutic interventions of a preventive nature.

(b) Further research is required to improve screening, with the intention of identifying children who are at high risk of adverse adult outcomes such as antisocial personality disorder, in order to target primary preventive interventions in these high-risk groups.

(c) There is currently a small number of ongoing longitudinal studies in the UK which might be exploited to answer a limited number of important research questions in this area.

(d) New longitudinal studies are urgently required which are specifically designed to answer more of the key questions which cannot be answered by the longitudinal studies that are already underway in the UK. These should be given high priority.

(e) Future longitudinal studies should include children from ethnic minorities and girls.

(f) More longitudinal research is required into offenders with borderline personality disorder. This is important in view of research which suggests that they may have a poor prognosis, especially as they occupy a significant number of beds in secure psychiatric hospitals (see Chapter 3).

(g) Child and adolescent mental health services will need to be appropriately resourced and equipped to provide preventive interventions at primary, secondary and tertiary level in children and adolescents identified as belonging to these high-risk groups.

5 Treatment and treatability of antisocial personality disorder

Executive summary

Findings from research into the treatment of offenders with personality disorders have limited value because of the methodology used, sample definitions and relatively short follow-up periods. Some observers believe that this accounts for the wide range of approaches currently available for the treatment of personality disorder and the differing views of authorities within the field of forensic psychiatry. Until sufficient evidence is available, preferably from randomised controlled trials, any recommendations made about the treatment or treatability of offenders with personality disorder will be provisional and subject to review. Until this evidence is available clinical risk assessment and management provide a pragmatic approach to meeting individual needs and minimising risk to the public. Some maintain that criminal recidivism may provide a good measure of outcome within psychiatric research, although this is still contentious. Psychiatric services in the UK were not set up to prevent criminal recidivism as a primary goal. A shift to the prevention of recidivism would require a shift in emphasis from delivery of care in the community to surveillance and social control.

While some psychiatrists remain keen to try to treat offenders with personality disorder, many hold a more pessimistic view about the success of treatment with this group.

With regard to in-patient services, because of hospital closures in the past decade, facilities (both secure and non-secure) are grossly over-crowded. The potential of these individuals to be disruptive and at times behave dangerously in hospital settings makes them increasingly unattractive to services that have progressively shifted their focus to the community. However, despite these real concerns, it remains clear that such patients do manifest severe psychological disturbance and that they frequently present to various health care agencies, or else behave in ways that will result in others having to intervene in their lives.

Treatment goals

Is it the primary intention to:

(a) Treat the personality disorder?
(b) Treat any other associated clinical syndrome?
(c) Improve the overall level of social functioning?
(d) Reduce the risk of physical harm to others?

If personality disorder is defined as an enduring pattern of perceiving, relating to, and thinking about the environment and oneself, exhibited in a range of social and personal contexts that are inflexible and pervasive, of stable and long duration, and with an onset in adolescence or early childhood, then it is also likely to be very difficult to treat. A significant proportion of patients may well show little or no improvement from any therapeutic endeavour. Most health care professionals might understandably as an alternative see their primary goal to be the treatment of associated clinical syndromes or take a selective approach to specific symptoms associated with certain less-treatable personality disorder categories as a more viable goal of treatment. Similarly, daily living skills, difficulties with interpersonal relationships, and problems in the area of quality of life might be seen as more reasonable goals for health care professionals to set when approaching patients with personality disorder.

The most frequently used measure of outcome in most studies of the treatment of offenders with personality disorder is reconviction (Dolan & Coid, 1993). However, two issues arise when considering this as an outcome measure; first, whether criminal behaviour is an appropriate measure of outcome, and second, whether it is an accurate measure of criminal behaviour. Robertson (1989) has suggested that the use of "criminological criteria to assess the usefulness of psychiatric intervention is ... mistaken in principle and impossible in practice". He notes that criteria to judge the success of treatment for patients with mental illness are the same for offenders and non-offenders, and are related to their psychiatric illness. In the case of individuals with a mental illness, the condition can remit or respond to treatment and mental state will be considered when making discharge decisions. However, for patients with personality disorder, where the validity of the medical concept remains dubious and the 'illness' remains undefined, the emphasis tends to be on criminal rather than clinical criteria. In this situation, the offence which may have led to admission will become the centre of discussions about the patient's discharge from a secure hospital setting (Robertson, 1992).

There is a problem in that any treatment effects may only be a very small factor among a multitude of additional circumstances upon which a reconviction will later depend once the patient is returned to the community. There is also the question of whether the offending behaviour will be detected and whether reconviction will ensue in a situation where it is detected. However, perhaps the most important consideration for psychiatrists is the attitude of the general public and the media and whether there are realistic expectations of psychiatric services regarding the prevention of re-offending. This is of special relevance where there has been a progressive change in the approach to the delivery of psychiatric services according to government policy, with a move to return patients to the community, and the abandonment in most psychiatric hospitals of a custodial regime. Thus, in secure forensic psychiatry services there is additional emphasis on security and protection of the public, while implementing therapeutic programmes. Implicit in such treatment programmes is the notion that the individual is likely to be returned to the community in the future. By further implication, reconviction will then imply therapeutic failure if external observers consider this the only goal of treatment and when the numerous external factors beyond the control of health care professionals in the community, which may contribute to the subsequent offence, are forgotten.

If the prevention of re-offending by individuals with personality disorder were to become the primary goal, there would need to be a fundamental change in the orientation and philosophy of mental health care services. Protection of the public would have to be emphasised to a considerably greater degree than is currently the case in clinical practice, more resources would be required, new legislation to intervene in patients' lives in the community would have to be enacted and new training would be necessary for the health care professionals involved. This would largely shift the balance within future interventions from treatment towards surveillance and social control. The likely impact on recruitment into this area of work would need to be considered seriously as health care professionals might well view this work as unattractive.

Risk management

The treatment of offenders with personality disorder should be directed by the risk management process which flows from the risk assessment referred to in Chapter 2. However, a particular problem in this field encountered by psychiatrists who are involved in the care of such individuals, both in hospital and especially in the community, is that it is impossible to attain zero risk. Risk management is about the identification and assessment of risks; it is a dynamic process as risks vary in terms of both quantity and quality over time. The management of risk can never be primarily led by objective risk assessment scales, which may be of use in large populations but have limitations when applied to individual cases. Risk assessment is a multi-disciplinary, multi-agency approach, which should allow a management plan to be put into place which will minimise risks to others.

It must be appreciated that however carefully risk has been managed, there is no certainty that tragic events will not occur.

Treatment studies

Most psychiatric research into the treatment of personality disorders has been carried out in in-patient settings and in prisons. Early writers on personality disorder were convinced that the condition could not be treated. This pessimism is not entirely justified, but a review by Dolan & Coid (1993) of research into treatment and management of antisocial and psychopathic disorder indicates that realistic expectations must be held of the success of therapeutic interventions with personality-disordered offenders.

Pharmacological treatment

Dolan & Coid (1993) highlighted two major questions posed by the pharmacological treatment of psychopathic disorder.

(a) Whether a condition that is composed of abnormal personality traits, rather than symptoms, can actually respond to medication.
(b) Whether any observed treatment response is confined exclusively to associated symptomatic conditions rather than core personality traits.

When taking a more flexible view, there are often no clear boundaries between abnormal personality traits and certain features of the major clinical syndromes of mental disorder. For example, many individuals with personality disorder show additional neurotic, affective, organic and at times psychotic symptoms, while not necessarily manifesting clinically recognisable diagnostic syndromes which could be classified as Axis I disorders. In a review of this complex area Docherty *et al* (1986) pointed out that the relationship between Axis II personality disorder and Axis I clinical syndromes becomes increasingly complex the closer it is examined. Thus, in view of the considerable comorbidity, it remains probable that these associated symptomatic components may show considerable potential for response to pharmacological agents.

The summary includes studies where the response of personality-disordered offenders has been examined using neuroleptics and antidepressants. To be included, each study had to have described the effects of the pharmacological agent on a patient or group of patients with a primary diagnosis of personality disorder.

Neuroleptic medication

Antipsychotic drugs have been recommended for many years in the treatment of personality disorders associated with aggression. Neuroleptics have both tranquillising effects on disturbed behaviour and a specific antipsychotic effect. There are few, if any, systematic trials of neuroleptic medication with patients diagnosed as having antisocial personality disorder, possibly because researchers may be deterred by accusations that tranquillising drugs would be used merely to control difficult behaviour, particularly in penal settings. However, lower doses of neuroleptics than would normally be prescribed for schizophrenia or depression may be helpful in the treatment of personality disorder, with some patients showing improvements in symptoms and behaviour. The side-effectsd of neuroleptics may result in poor compliance, along with a high drop-out rate, which reinforces the importance of administering neuroleptics in low doses when using them to treat individuals with personality disorder.

Previous placebo-controlled trials have consistently indicated greater improvement in symptoms considered to be on the borderline of schizophrenia, in particular schizotypal features. However, a more recent study examining the effect of haloperidol failed to find any improvement compared with placebo, and showed an overall inferiority on measures of depression, borderline psycho-pathological symptoms and anxiety compared with phenelzine (Soloff *et al*, 1993). Hence, Soloff *et al* concluded that they had failed to replicate prior results (including their own) on the efficacy of this neuroleptic on a broad spectrum of affective, schizotypal and behavioural symptoms. However, two important factors in this study may have influenced the overall negative findings. First, significantly more subjects with a history of depressive disorder were allocated by chance to the group receiving haloperidol. Second, the daily dose of haloperidol was low compared both with the usual clinical dose and with the dose used in their previous study (Soloff *et al*, 1986).

Antidepressants

Studies suggest that patients with a combination of affective disorder and personality disorder have a poorer response to antidepressant treatment than patients with affective disorders alone (Soloff, 1994). In addition, worsening of both affective symptoms and behaviour has been observed in a subgroup of patients with personality disorder treated with antidepressants. There have not been any trials of antidepressant medication which have been specifically applied to people with antisocial personality disorder. However, the response of borderline personality disorder (which has an affective component among its criteria) has been studied in a small number of open and placebo-controlled trials.

Other pharmacological interventions that have been used to treat personality disorder include: monoamine oxidase inhibitors, benzodiazepines, anticonvulsants, psychostimulants and lithium.

Physical treatment

Some researchers maintain that brain abnormality is a major aetiological factor in psychopathic behaviour, and such views have supported the investigation of physical treatments such as electroconvulsive therapy (ECT), cold wet sheet packs (Ross *et al*, 1988) and psychosurgery. However, many of these studies investigating physical treatments have produced inconclusive results: in a review of ECT studies, McCord (1982) concludes that the lack of clear positive results is unsurprising, as ECT served only to reduce anxiety, which is not a problem for many people with antisocial personality disorder. However, ECT may be useful in certain circumstances, such as when a person with a psychopathic disorder develops a severe depressive illness.

Falconer & Shur's (1959) review of studies of various psycho-surgical procedures carried out on personality-disordered individuals concluded that no firm conclusions could be reached about the success of these procedures, or about the justification of psychosurgery for these patients, until long-term follow-up studies were available. Since then there have been no long-term controlled trials of psychosurgery as a treatment for personality disorder or for aggressive behaviour and there is still no clear justification for its use.

Psychotherapies

Individual and group psychotherapy

Reports of out-patient psychotherapy are mostly of enforced or imposed treatments (Reckless, 1970; Carney, 1977) and have shown some limited success. Most psychotherapeutic treatment for offenders with personality disorder is carried out on an in-patient basis, mainly because the subjects are residing in prison or special hospitals. Some psychiatrists are pessimistic about the use of both group and individual psychotherapy, even within these structured environments. It could be said that, to some extent, this cynical attitude is justified; drop-out rates are often high, and there is often no marked long-term improvement following the programme.

Stein & Brown (1991) reported on group therapy with forensic patients who had committed violent crimes and were serving indeterminate sentences in a Canadian high security hospital. They noted the inability of their patients to form a cohesive group or to develop the group dynamics which help other types of patients (Yalom, 1975). Although 23% of the patients had a diagnosis of antisocial personality disorder and 16% had other personality disorders, 53% of the group also had a diagnosis of psychosis. Hence, it may have been that the heterogeneity of the sample diminished the possibility of group cohesion.

In contrast, working with patients with personality disorder on an individual basis has its own problems. The 'one-to-one' setting potentially enables the patients to manipulate the therapist and feign improvements. In group settings defensive tactics are more readily confronted by the therapist and other patients and the group may have less tolerance of attempts at manipulation (Carney, 1972; Borriello, 1979).

Despite the above, a certain amount of treatment success has been reported, particularly in terms of recidivism. For example, Jew *et al* (1972) evaluated group therapy with 257 male offenders with personality disorder. All subjects were given psycho-analytically-oriented sessions for a minimum of one year for eight hours a week. The men were matched on criminological and demographic factors judged to relate to recidivism with 257 men also in the prison at the same time who did not receive therapy. The rate of parole revocation during their first year on parole for the treated men was significantly lower than for the untreated offenders (25 *v.* 40%). However, the difference in number of returns to prison disappeared on a four-year follow-up. Jew *et al* (1972) attribute this re-offending to a lack of support facilities for men on parole.

Although these results are promising in terms of recidivism, there are methodological shortcomings, particularly the very short follow-up periods. Hence, although significant effects of treatment are found at six months or a year after therapy or release, those studies which have gone on to follow their subjects for longer periods find that the effect diminishes over time. In addition, for psychotherapy to be successful, some continuation of support or contact after treatment may be important to help prevent relapse. There are, however, no empirical studies that have considered the after-care needed to maintain improvements after any type of psychotherapy.

Cognitive–behavioural therapy

Cognitive–behavioural therapy is being used to treat a wide range of psychiatric disorders at present. Although it is sometimes thought of as an individual treatment, it has to be modified considerably for different populations and is perhaps best summarised as a treatment approach rather than a specific therapy. It is also important to realise that any treatment needs to be evaluated over a long time-scale before it can be regarded as effective in terms of personality disorder outcome.

There are some encouraging recent developments. In a single case study series, Davidson & Tyrer (1996) showed that cognitive therapy was of value to patients with borderline and antisocial personality disorders when focused on specific behaviours directly linked to personality disturbance, and administered using a flexible timescale over a period of about six months. Particularly in the treatment and prevention of aggression, cognitive therapy may be valuable in breaking the links between the antecedents of aggressive behaviour and violent acts. Altered cognitions may be able to prevent the expression of aggression, and this deserves further development in therapeutic approaches (Alpet & Spillman, 1997).

Therapeutic community approach

There have been many studies of the efficacy of the therapeutic community approach to mentally disordered offenders since the first report of its value in 1948. Unfortunately, its value in the treatment of mentally disordered offenders is still open to dispute because of the absence of controlled therapeutic interventions, the tendency for patients with better outcomes to be selected for the treatment programme, and the limited length of follow-up. The best evidence of its value has come from recent studies at the Henderson Hospital in Surrey. For nearly 50 years the Henderson Hospital has run a democratic therapeutic community where patients with personality disorder are closely involved in the day-to-day running of their community and in the selection of new residents. Comparison of those who are taken on for care with those who are not considered (mainly because of funding difficulties) suggests that, in the year after treatment, those in the therapeutic community may require much less in-patient care and save a great deal on costs (Dolan *et al*, 1996, 1997). The patients chosen for treatment have severe personality disorder which in research terms is not fully defined, but they have an average of four DSM/ICD personality disorder diagnoses and are clearly a disturbed population. However, most have borderline personality disorder and their disturbed behaviour is often directed towards themselves (i.e. self-harm). Serious offenders whose behaviour is overtly challenging and disruptive are not taken on for treatment by the Henderson system.

The Henderson Hospital approach is currently expanding in the UK and two further centres are being opened (in South Birmingham and Salford) within the next year. This will establish for the first time a nationwide service for a selected group of individuals with severe personality disorder but will not provide a solution to the needs of more than a small minority of offenders with personality disorder.

'Milieu' therapy

A striking feature of reports of outcome after long-term in-patient treatment in hospitals is that, with few exceptions, the actual treatment received by patients is not described. Treatment is often described as milieu therapy which, as Blackburn (1992) points out, is usually a euphemism for an orderly regime within the hospital. Milieu therapy offered within secure and non-secure hospitals includes pharmaco-therapy, psychotherapy, occupational therapy, cognitive therapy, group therapy, behavioural therapy and social skills training. These elements of therapy are delivered by a range of staff from differing professional backgrounds who are often operating within different conceptual frameworks and applying different models of treatment to one aspect, behavioural feature or symptom of the patient.

Follow-up studies in the more secure environments of special hospitals suggest that, for some patients detained under the Mental Health Act psychopathic disorder category, hospital admission results in a reduction in offending. Although the 'success' rate is poorer than that found for patients with a mental illness, around 50% of people with antisocial personality disorder do not re-offend within three years, and serious violent offences are committed by only a quarter of those released. The lack of attention given to the actual treatment received by these patients makes commenting on the efficacy of specific treatment methods impossible. No controlled studies of treatment versus non-treatment, or comparing two different treatment approaches, are available, so it cannot be assumed that it is the therapy rather than the passage of time that is effecting change.

Milieu therapy in non-British high security settings has also shown some improvement in inmates' recidivism following incarceration. The Patuxent Institution in the USA and Herstedvester in Denmark are roughly equivalent to British special hospitals in that they detain patients with psychopathic disorders for indeterminate treatment under the relevant mental health legislation of the country or state. However, they are seen as part of the prison service rather than the health services. These institutions have shown that those men who complete treatment have a significantly lower reconviction rate than men 'partially' treated or referred 'untreated' because of legal decisions. However, the factors contributing to some men not having a full course of treatment before release from Patuxent may also be correlated with re-offending. In Denmark, Herstedvester has also suggested good outcome results, but again no controlled trials are available. The patients at the English special hospitals and at Patuxent and Herstedvester may represent some of the most difficult offenders with antisocial personality disorders to control within a conventional system and those most likely to re-offend. Without appropriate descriptions of treatment and randomised controlled trials, however, conclusions about the efficacy of the institutions must remain guarded.

Community supervision

It is probably more appropriate to classify community supervision as a form of patient management than as a treatment modality. Nevertheless, analyses of research into the effects of community surveillance of offenders as a condition of their release from prison (Palmer, 1992) and of conditions of supervision of patients discharged from high security hospitals (MacCulloch & Bailey, 1993) suggest that community supervision could act as an essential adjunct to treatment programmes for offenders with personality disorder. When evaluating any programme of community supervision it must be determined at the outset exactly what the supervision entailed and what the ultimate goals of the programme were. Additionally, it must be questioned whether health care professionals are the best individuals to conduct such programmes. Questions arise about whether the programme primarily involves surveillance as an alternative to institutionalisation, but still involves significant punitive or restrictive elements, or whether it is primarily designed to be rehabilitative. Community supervision of offenders with personality disorder cannot be fruitfully considered unless this dichotomy is understood. Furthermore, official pressures on professionals involved in supervision may be in one direction, while their personal goals of clinical management may be quite different.

Hann *et al* (1991) have reviewed a number of research studies from Canada, the USA and the UK which suggest that offenders granted parole were reconvicted less often than those for whom parole was not granted, when parole involved supervised release on license of prisoners before the expiry of the sentence. No studies have specifically set out to evaluate whether offenders with personality disorder released into the community and allocated to community supervision or a control form of management (or simply no supervision at all) have a better outcome at follow-up. However, in Britain legislative powers under the Mental Health Act 1983 allow for compulsory supervision of individuals with personality disorder under the terms of Section 41. There is some evidence that patients who have be en detained under these conditions and who have a high risk of re-offending are less likely to re-offend in the two years after discharge when receiving community supervision than those who receive no supervision at all (Walker & McCabe, 1973). A more recent study has reported a positive effect of conditional discharge of patients from special hospitals in terms of serious recidivism rates when both mentally ill patients and those with antisocial personality disorder were analysed together (Bailey & MacMulloch, 1992*a,b*).The significant effect of community supervision was not found when the results for the patients with antisocial personality disorder were re-analysed separately.

Recommendations and conclusions

(a) The current goals of treatment for offenders with personality disorder are ill-defined and require further refinement.

(b) No treatment can be regarded as effective in offenders with personality disorder until it has been tested in a controlled trial, with independent (blind or masked) assessment.

(c) There is an urgent need for clinical trials, based on random allocation and with long-term follow-up, of therapeutic regimes designed to change the behaviour of people with antisocial personality disorders.

(d) A review of treatments of adult offenders with personality disorder indicates some modest benefits from therapeutic community approaches, both in prison and hospital in-patient settings. However, these therapeutic interventions are limited by their inherent requirement that patients should enter voluntarily into these programmes. When developing new services, planners should be aware that these programmes are highly selective and will exclude a high proportion of offenders with personality disorder.

(e) Pharmacological studies have demonstrated encouraging results and further research is needed in this area. Most have included individuals with borderline rather than antisocial personality disorders and those presenting with associated clinical symptoms.

6   Primary prevention

Executive summary

There should now be further research into primary preventive interventions in childhood. There are a number of encouraging findings using a range of different techniques. It remains unclear whether primary intervention programmes are capable of preventing the development of the most severe and persistent antisocial behaviour in adulthood and the most adverse outcomes such as antisocial and borderline personality disorders. Furthermore, primary prevention strategies will require long-term evaluation. In the meantime, however, the preventive approach appears to offer more hope and a stronger basis for the investment of scarce resources, especially as the benefits of treatment interventions for adults are modest or equivocal.

A review of therapeutic interventions for adult offenders with personality disorder does not make a strong case for any individual treatment modality demonstrating more than moderate effectiveness, and then only in selected samples (Dolan & Coid, 1993). Longitudinal studies of individuals with borderline and antisocial personality disorders suggest that these conditions are likely to be exceptionally hard to treat and that some cases will be unresponsive to all therapeutic endeavours. While it can be argued that further research is needed into treatment interventions for adults with personality disorders who offend, it must also be questioned whether there should now be a major shift in emphasis. We therefore argue that primary preventive interventions in childhood should now be targeted for further research and development.

It is important to be clear, however, what form of prevention is intended. For example, in the prevention of criminal behaviour, four types of prevention can be distinguished (Tonry & Farrington, 1995). Criminal justice prevention refers to traditional deterrence, such as incapacitation and rehabilitation strategies operated by law enforcement and criminal justice agencies. Situational prevention refers to interventions designed to reduce the opportunities for antisocial behaviour and to increase the barriers to the committing of antisocial acts. Community prevention refers to interventions designed to change the social conditions and social institutions (e.g. community norms in organisations) that influence antisocial behaviour in communities. Developmental prevention refers to interventions that are designed to mould the development of behaviour in individuals by working on the risk and protective factors influencing human development. Primary prevention of personality disorder is part of the latter approach taken by criminologists, in which emphasis is placed on the longitudinal developmental course of individuals presenting with known precursors of adult antisocial behaviour, thereby targeting high-risk individuals.

Research into early prevention

Research into early prevention has tended to study specific outcomes such as juvenile delinquency or adult crime. Few studies have assessed the effects of prevention programmes on the most pathological examples of antisocial behaviour. They have concentrated instead on a full range of variation. Furthermore, most research is focused on males. It must also be pointed out that programmes aiming to prevent antisocial behaviour should ideally be based on empirically validated theories about the causes of that behaviour. Such a theoretical approach is largely absent from this area of study. Consequently, the most useful prevention techniques tend to be risk-focused ones that aim to tackle numerous factors.

A primary preventive approach could have three possible goals, although few programmes have specifically identified these as their aims. These might include the following.

Prevention of the development of conduct disorder

It has been shown that a subgroup of children with conduct disorder will persist in their antisocial behaviour and develop an antisocial personality disorder in adulthood. Programmes could be devised that prevent children developing this precursor of the adult antisocial syndrome in the first place.

Increasing the rate of 'drop-outs'

Programmes could be devised which are intended to increase the rate at which children who are identified as having conduct disorder drop-out before progressing to the adult syndrome of antisocial personality disorder. This approach would target children with conduct disorder, but would cover a range of behavioural problems and levels of severity among the children selected.

Targeted approach

A highly targeted approach would involve the selection of a subgroup of children who were identified as being most at risk. For example, those above a threshold for a number of specific conduct-disordered behaviours, or behaviours considered to be most serious or most accurately predictive of future antisocial personality disorder, with a commitment to continued input during adolescence and into early adulthood to manage risk and maximise potential for positive change.

Prevention of inter-generational transmission

Programmes could be devised to target children in high-risk families demonstrating signs of conduct disorder, using a multi-disciplinary, multi-agency approach, supportive of families and parents.

Pregnancy and infancy programmes

Problems in pregnancy and infancy can be alleviated by home visiting programmes designed to help mothers. A study in New York State randomly allocated 400 mothers to receive home visits from nurses during pregnancy, to visits both during pregnancy and during the first two years of the child's life, or to a control group who received no visits (Olds *et al*, 1986*a,b*). Home visitors gave advice about prenatal and postnatal care, infant development and the importance of proper nutrition and avoiding smoking and drinking during pregnancy. Home visits led to teenage mothers having heavier babies, fewer preterm deliveries and a decrease in smoking by the mothers. Postnatal home visits appeared to result in a decrease in recorded child physical abuse and neglect during the first two years of life, especially by poor, unmarried, teenage mothers.

The Syracuse New York Family Development Research Programme carried out research with a sample of pregnant women and gave them weekly help with child-rearing, health, nutrition and other problems, and collected outcome data on delinquency (Lally *et al*, 1988). In addition, the children received free day care designed to develop their intellectual abilities up to the age of eight years. This was not a randomised experiment but matched controls were chosen when the children were aged three years. Treated subjects had significantly higher intelligence than controls at age three, but were not different at age five. However, at a mean age of 15, significantly fewer of the treated children (2 *v.* 17%) had been referred to a juvenile court for delinquency and treated girls showed better school attendance and school performance.

Pre-school programmes

The Perry Pre-School Project carried out in Michigan involved a 'head start' programme targeting disadvantaged African–American children who were allocated to experimental and control groups (Schweinhart & Weikart, 1980). Experimental children attended a daily pre-school programme backed-up by weekly home visits, usually lasting two years, covering ages 3–4 years. The aim was to provide intellectual stimulation, increase thinking and reasoning abilities, and to increase later school achievement. When followed-up at age 15, the experimental group showed gains in intelligence that were, in fact, short-lived. However, they were significantly better when rated for elementary school motivation, school achievement at age 14, teacher ratings of classroom behaviour at 6–9 years, self-reports of classroom behaviour at 15 and self-reports of offending at 15. When followed up at age 19, the experimental group were more likely to be employed and to have graduated from high school, more likely to have received college or vocational training and less likely to have been arrested (Berrueta-Clement *et al*, 1984). By the age of 27, the experimental group had accumulated only half as many arrests on average as the control subjects, had significantly higher earnings and were more likely to be home owners. More women from the experimental group were married and fewer of their children had been born out of wedlock (Schweinhart *et al*, 1993).

Parenting programmes

Kazdin (1987) reviewed a series of family approaches to the treatment of antisocial behaviour in children. Behavioural parent management programmes developed by Patterson (1982) in Oregon showed promising results. Careful observations of parent–child interactions demonstrated that the parents of children with antisocial behaviour were deficient in methods of child-rearing. They tended to fail in telling their children how they were expected to behave, monitoring in behaviour to ensure that it was desirable and enforcing rules promptly and unambiguously with appropriate rewards and penalties.

They used more punishment, but failed to make it contingent on the child's behaviour. Patterson attempted to train parents in more effective child-rearing methods. His treatment has been shown to be effective in reducing stealing and other antisocial behaviour in children over short periods in small-scale studies (Dishion *et al*, 1992; Patterson *et al*, 1992).

Skills training

Cognitive–behavioural interpersonal skills training has been used in an attempt to reduce impulsivity. Reviews of delinquency rehabilitation programmes suggest that those which were successful in reducing offending generally tried to change the offenders' thinking (Gendreau & Ross, 1979, 1987). In a 'reasoning and rehabilitation' programme in Ottawa, Ross and colleagues carried out a randomised trial that led to a significant (74%) decrease in re-offending for a small sample over a short nine-month follow-up period where training was carried out by probation officers (Ross *et al*, 1988; Ross & Ross, 1988). The programme aimed to modify the impulsive, egocentric thinking of delinquents and to teach them to stop and think before acting, to consider the consequences of their behaviour, conceptualise alternative ways of solving interpersonal problems and to consider the impact of their behaviour on other people, especially victims.

Peer programmes

Several studies have demonstrated that school children can be taught to resist peer influences which encourage smoking, drinking and marijuana use (Telch *et al*, 1982; Murray *et al*, 1984; Botvin *et al*, 1990; Hawkins *et al*, 1991). A large-scale meta-analysis of 143 substance use programmes by Tobler (1986) also concluded that programmes using peer leaders were the most effective in reducing smoking, drinking and drug use. Similar techniques designed to counter antisocial peer pressures might be developed in the future to decrease antisocial behaviour.

School programmes

School-based programmes have concentrated successfully on decreasing bullying. Farrington (1993) has observed the strong link between bullying and other types of antisocial behaviour. Olweus (1993, 1994) implemented an anti-bullying programme in Norway aimed at increasing the awareness and knowledge of teachers, parents and children about bullying and to dispel myths about it. A booklet and a video about bullying were made available to schools together with a folder for parents containing information and advice. Anonymous self-report questionnaires were completed by children in 42 participating schools to provide information on the prevalence of bullies and victims. During the programme, teachers were encouraged to develop rules about bullying and to discuss bullying in class, using the video and role-playing exercises. Teachers were also encouraged to improve monitoring and supervision of children, especially in the playground. The programme was successful in reducing the prevalence of bullying by half.

A similar programme introduced in 23 Sheffield schools by Smith & Sharp (1994) had considerable success in reducing bullying in primary schools but relatively small effects in secondary schools.

Multiple component programmes

A combination of therapeutic interventions may be more effective than a single method. This has been observed in the case of adult offenders with antisocial and psychopathic personality disorders by Dolan & Coid (1993). Tremblay *et al* (1991, 1992) targeted disruptive (aggressive/hyperactive) boys at age six for a prevention experiment in Montreal. Between the ages of seven and nine years, the experimental group received training to foster social skills and self-control. Parents were also trained using the Parent Management Training Techniques developed by Patterson (1982). By the age of 12, those in the experimental group had committed fewer burglaries and thefts, were less likely to get drunk and less likely to get involved in fights than the controls. They also had higher school achievement. Differences in antisocial behaviour between experimental and control subjects also appeared to increase as the follow-up progressed.

A study in Seattle combined parent training, teacher training and skills training in a school-based prevention experiment (Hawkins *et al*, 1991). Children in the experimental group received special treatment both at home and at school designed to increase attachment to their parents and bonding to the school, based on the hypothesis that offending was inhibited by the strength of social bonds. Parents were trained to notice and reinforce socially desirable behaviour and teachers were trained in classroom management to provide clear

instructions and expectations to children, reward them for particip-
ation in desired behaviour and teach acceptable socially desirable
methods of solving problems (Hawkins *et al*, 1988). Eighteen months
later, boys who participated in the programme were significantly less
aggressive than controls according to teacher ratings, the difference
being more marked for White than African–American boys. Girls in
the experimental group were not less aggressive but were found to be
less self-destructive, anxious and depressed. When assessed at 10 years
old, the children in the experimental group were less likely to have
initiated delinquency and alcohol use.

Community programmes

A promising risk-focused prevention programme entitled 'Communities that Care' has been developed that is tailored to the needs of
individual communities (Hawkins & Catalano, 1992). The programme
is flexible in that a 'community' could be a city, county, small town or
even a housing estate. The programme aims to reduce delinquency
and drug use by implementing prevention strategies that have
demonstrated effectiveness in reducing particular risk factors. This is
modelled on large-scale community-wide public health programmes
designed to reduce illnesses such as coronary heart disease by tackling
risk factors such as smoking, poor diet and lack of exercise. The
programme begins with 'community mobilisation' where key leaders
are brought together with the aim of getting them to agree on the
goals of the programme and to implement it. The key leaders then set
up a 'community board' that is accountable to them, consisting of
representatives from various agencies. The board then carries out a
risk assessment, identifying key risk factors in that particular community
that need to be tackled. This may involve the use of police, school,
social or census records or local surveys. After identifying the risk
factors, the board then develops a prevention plan of strategies to
combat the risk factors. The choice of strategies is based on empirical
evidence about what is effective and depends on what are identified as
the biggest problems in the community. In developing the prevention
plan, the community board may also have to develop methods of
funding and supporting its implementation. If necessary, technical
assistance can be provided to train the implementers. Implementation
is monitored in the process of evaluation and the effectiveness is
assessed in an outcome evaluation. The success of the programme
has not yet been rigorously evaluated, but there are current plans
to implement and evaluate a similar programme in the UK
(Farrington, 1997).

Recommendations and conclusions

(a) Studies of longitudinal development suggest that certain patterns of antisocial behaviour may be highly resistant to change by early adulthood. There should now be a shift in emphasis towards research into the development of primary prevention strategies for adult antisocial behaviour and personality disorder which involve children and adolescents.

(b) It may be preferable when developing these therapeutic interventions to concentrate on those which include multiple components.

(c) Research is needed to identify the stages of childhood development at which primary preventive intervention strategies are likely to have their optimum benefit.

(d) Intervention programmes will require long-term evaluation. Few will deliver useful results in the short term.

(e) There is also a need to ensure the safe transition of services from adolescence to adulthood.

7   Current context

Executive summary

As part of government policy, psychiatric services in the UK have progressively relocated the focus for the delivery of care from hospitals to the community. Few in-patient facilities are now able safely to contain offenders with personality disorder – except for high security hospitals – and few psychiatrists see themselves as having any role in the compulsory admission of these individuals for treatment in psychiatric hospitals. Nevertheless, the Mental Health Act 1983 does give psychiatrists considerable powers to detain patients with personality disorder if they require treatment and are likely to respond. As criminal law in the UK does not permit either the arrest of individuals on the grounds that they might in the future pose a danger to the public, or the preventive detention of high-risk individuals already in prison, politicians and members of the public frequently look to mental health legislation as a means of filling this vacuum. Psychiatrists cannot successfully treat the majority of high-risk individuals with personality disorder and no longer have the resources to detain them. Cost-effectiveness also has to be borne in mind when considering future placements for offenders with personality disorder. Research should be undertaken to compare the cost-effectiveness of secure hospital care with other methods of management, such as detention in prison.

Many psychiatrists in the UK now question their role in the compulsory admission of offenders with personality disorder. Whereas approximately 25% of patients in the special hospitals are detained under the legal category of psychopathic disorder (Hamilton, 1990), the proportion drops to a mere 0.24% among those compulsorily admitted to ordinary National Health Service (NHS) facilities in England and Wales (Government Statistical Service, 1991). This is, at least in part, because it has become increasingly difficult to contain offender patients safely in NHS facilities as district health authorities have progressively closed down locked facilities over the past two decades and dismantled structured regimes that could have provided long-term care, and had until recently embraced the policy of care in the community. Other health care professionals, politicians, the public, probation services, police, prison staff and other statutory and non-governmental organisations hold and debate differing views of the role and responsibility of psychiatrists in the assessment, care and treatment of offenders with personality disorders. They frequently complain that they have to shoulder the burden of a group of people who display a level of psychological disturbance such that they seem to them to be clearly mentally disordered, but whom psychiatrists do not accept as patients. The public has become increasingly sensitised following highly publicised escapes from secure hospitals, homicides committed soon after discharge from hospital and other pathways involving dangerous patients. Being denied admission to hospital after being deemed 'untreatable' by a psychiatrist according to clauses under the legal category of psychopathic disorder of the Mental Health Act 1983 has been followed on occasions by further serious offending and subsequent political and media attention, suggesting that if psychiatrists had intervened, then the offence would not have occurred.

This raises the question of whether there is a genuine case for hospital treatment and supervision in the community for offenders with personality disorder who may be dangerous. The answer is not straightforward because account must be taken of both the fact that many patients with personality disorders do not show much sustained response to conventional psychiatric interventions (see Chapter 5) and the ongoing difficulty of shortage of appropriate resources. Nevertheless, patients with personality disorder are regularly admitted on an informal basis to hospital despite the reluctance of psychiatrists. Such patients are often in crises after deliberate self-harm, substance misuse and other impulsive behaviours, and Chapter 3 has demonstrated that patients with conditions such as borderline personality disorder are frequently admitted because of their high levels of help-seeking behaviour.

Many of these patients are also prone to recurrent episodes of serious mental disorder over their lifetime (Coid, 1992). These treatable conditions inevitably place a high demand on psychiatric services, even if the underlying abnormality of their personality will ultimately remain unresponsive. In-patient treatment is notoriously difficult and can be physically and emotionally hazardous to other patients and to staff. An ability to split staff teams (Strasburger, 1986) and induce profound counter-transference reaction (Symington, 1980) is well known. For those who attempt to manage the most difficult and dangerous cases the price may be too high. In Scotland, the murders committed by two people with antisocial personality disorder who escaped from the State Hospital of Carstairs led to a total collapse of staff morale and the locking out of the physician superintendent (Scottish Home & Health Department, 1977). The Fallon Inquiry (Department of Health, 1999) was set up more recently in order to investigate the alarming situation that had developed in the Personality Disorder Unit at Ashworth High Security Hospital.

Because offenders with personality disorder have a higher risk of re-offending than other patients when released from hospital, psychiatrists need to be wary of accepting more responsibility than can realistically be taken and should not admit them to in-patient facilities that are inadequate for safe management. Although we have demonstrated that treatment does help a number of these individuals, doctors who retain any interest in this problem may be taking a serious risk with their reputations if therapeutic success is measured only in terms of re-offending behaviour after discharge. Psychiatrists' morale has been badly damaged in recent years by the establishment of mandatory inquiries into suicides and homicides. These are unlikely to encourage new members of the profession to take responsibility for the highest-risk group of patients and to take on a primary public protection role. It would be a brave psychiatrist working outside a high security hospital who would take on the responsibility for a specialist service (in-patient and community care) for offenders with personality disorder in the current political climate. The Mental Health Act 1983 places responsibilities on psychiatrists that in many cases cannot now be fulfilled. Psychiatrists and patients may both be caught in a dilemma because no-one would be likely to want to take responsibility for an unacceptable risk if there were new proposals to increase the rate of transfer of offenders with personality disorder from prison for periods of treatment under the Mental Health Act in secure hospitals. The covert political pressures to continue to detain those who were dangerous after the expected date of their release would have to be removed. An alternative to detention in hospital without a time limit and when no effective treatment can be given, but where the patient remains potentially dangerous, will also have to found. It is becoming increasingly important that psychiatrists inform other professionals, the media and the public about what can realistically be achieved by treatment, and that psychiatric hospitals have long ceased to be places that can provide long-term custodial care.

Other professions, such as probation officers and members of the Parole Board, accept the risk that a proportion of their service users will re-offend and that these re-offenders will attract public opprobrium or disciplinary measures. The Royal College of Psychiatrists has recommended the risk assessment of patients on a routine basis and has issued guidance (Royal College of Psychiatrists, 1996). However, this must be placed firmly in perspective. Merely carrying out a risk assessment does not guarantee the removal of risk and, even when risk is identified, resources may not be adequate in many locations to reduce that risk.

Current legislation

Although it has been possible to issue clear instructions for good practice to guide professionals on intervention, their limitations must be recognised. Most dangerous patients do not readily accept supervision or treatment in the community and the current Care Programme Approach within mental health services will reduce risk only in those who are willing to cooperate in its implementation. Similarly, merely placing patients on a computerised register will not in itself ensure the public safety. Assertive outreach programmes aim to reduce violence by high-risk patients (Droskin & Steadman, 1994), but have not yet demonstrated their effectiveness in the UK. They would require considerable investment and new resources and may not be adequately funded except in a handful of model community services in districts where overall service demands are low.

The Government has recently established a working party to review mental health legislation under the chairmanship of Professor Genevra Richardson (Department of Health press release R1199–06: "Expert advisor appointed to start review of Mental Health Act", 17 September 1998). At present, coercive treatment with recall to hospital is permitted only after the event of serious, dangerous behaviour, and the imposition of a restriction order under Section 41 in a Crown Court. Recommendations of increased powers of supervision and recall to hospital of patients residing in the community were rejected by the previous government after legal advice that forcing treatment in the community, other than under a restriction order, would contravene Article 5 of the European Convention of Human Rights (Department of Health, 1993). Unfortunately, the Mental Health (Patients in the Community) Act 1995 provides no effective power of intervention and has been criticised as being clinically irrelevant when legal control of treatment and living arrangements cannot be extended into the community (Eastman, 1997).

The Department of Health's guidelines for the care and treatment of discharged patients (Department of Health, 1994) have diverted attention from several of the key issues. A subgroup of severely mentally ill individuals and those with personality disorders pose an increased risk to the community and many of these people have concurrent illicit drug and alcohol dependency problems. Effective clinical intervention and the parallel prevention of dangerous behaviour continue to be guided by policies which emphasise bureaucratic procedures, in a situation in which resources for community supervision are inadequate and where legislation is ineffective. However, if new legislation is to be introduced, it must be questioned whether the current resources, most importantly the number of acute admission beds in psychiatric hospitals, would be adequate to cope with the inevitable demand that would be created by the new legislation. This situation would be worst in the very areas that require the most resources, such as inner cities and other socio-economically deprived areas. It is in these locations that the demand for beds is highest from offender patients and where there is currently no adequate system of resource allocation to redress inequity (further details available from Professor Coid upon request).

One additional legislative issue that should not be forgotten is that the Mental Health Act 1983 is the only legislation in England and Wales that permits an individual to be detained against his or her will on the basis of what he or she might do in the future. Uniquely, the Mental Health Act allows individuals to be detained on the basis of their potential dangerousness. Criminal law does not allow members of the public to be arrested in such circumstances and this can occur only after the event of a suspected criminal offence. However, mental health legislation permits detention only in circumstances where a psychiatrist has diagnosed the presence of mental disorder, and in these circumstances the legislation is expressly for the purpose of observation, assessment and/or treatment of the patient's mental disorder.

The Mental Health Act goes further in that, under Part II, individuals can be detained if a psychiatrist considers that they are in need of treatment. It is not always necessary to demonstrate dangerousness and, as an alternative, self-neglect or the possibility of self-harm can be grounds for detention. Mental health legislation also permits detention in hospital with further extensions, provided that treatment is for the patient's mental disorder. Thus, in the absence of alternative legislation that can remove individuals from the community who are considered to pose a risk to the public, and where the preventive detention of high-risk individuals in prison is no longer on the statutes, there can be subtle pressures on psychiatrists to operate the Mental Health Act in order to fill this vacuum. Difficulties arise when behaviour that is considered to be dangerous or high-risk appears to indicate to the public, politicians and the media that the individual suffers from some form of mental disorder. Furthermore, certain criteria for categories of personality disorder include impulsive, violent, criminal and high-risk behaviours. The question is inevitably posed that if an individual is presenting with signs or symptoms that are akin to, or actually comprise, components of a recognised form of mental disorder, then the psychiatrist should act (or, after the event of a serious offence, should have acted) to protect the public by compulsorily detaining that individual in hospital with a view to treating this condition. (Whether the condition in question was necessarily related to the high-risk behaviour may be ignored when public perception of risk is involved.)

The use of mental health legislation has proved irresistible to politicians in the USA when faced with public outrage over the risk posed by certain offenders released into the community, especially paedophiles and other serious sexual offenders (Fitch, 1998). Some states have enacted legislation which allows courts to send individuals with sexual deviations to hospital for prolonged compulsory treatment, irrespective of whether they wish to cooperate or are likely to benefit. This legislation has often targeted convicted offenders who have completed criminal sentences and are about to be released from confinement, significantly extending the reach of civil commitment.

Costs of treating offenders with personality disorder

The potential costs of treating offenders with personality disorder in different illustrations are compared in Table 7.1, and there is considerable variation between different settings. For example, the costs of in-patient secure care for mentally disordered offenders are high, especially in medium secure units, and compare unfavourably with the average of £61 per day that it costs to treat a patient with schizophrenia in the community (Guest *et al*, 1996). This difference in cost has two major implications. First, there is considerable scope for perverse financial incentives to prevent individuals moving from one level to another. The chances of this happening are increased when funding bodies who would have to bear the increased costs of any move have a direct input into the decision over whether an offender with personality disorder can change from one level of security to another, or one institution to another. Second, differences in cost increase the pressure on health care professionals to demonstrate value for money. It can be argued, though, that this is an entirely appropriate form of evaluation of health care services. The modest effectiveness of the wide range of interventions that we have reviewed in Chapter 5 must inevitably cause policy-makers and managers to question the use of these expensive and scarce resources for patients who are likely to show only limited benefit.

TABLE 7.1
Approximate costs of treating mentally disordered offenders in different settings

Setting	Approximate cost per patient per year (£)
Medium secure – independent sector	80 000–150 000
Medium secure – NHS	100 000–110 000
High security	100 000
Prison (general)	25 000–30 000
Grendon Prison	26 000
Therapeutic community	39 960[1]

1. Assuming a linear trend and based on £23 310 for an average stay of seven months (Menzies *et al*, 1993)

Recommendations and conclusions

(a) It has become increasingly important to make the public aware that the closure of psychiatric hospitals, and hence of regimes that could in the past have contained offenders with personality disorder, has been dictated by government policy. It is unrealistic to expect psychiatrists to manage such individuals safely in community-based services.

(b) It should be noted that mental health legislation does empower psychiatrists to detain offenders with personality disorder in hospital under the legal category of psychopathic disorder. However, the Mental Health Act 1983 stipulates that this can only be in circumstances where the individual requires treatment and when the treatment offered is likely "to alleviate or prevent a deterioration" of the patient's condition.

(c) It is the responsibility of psychiatrists to offer treatment wherever possible, including for patients needing to be held in conditions of security, under the Mental Health Act, when they are deemed to be a danger to themselves or others. It is not part of the responsibility of psychiatry to detain patients without any prospect of effective treatment.

(d) Any new legislation to protect the public from high-risk offenders with personality disorder, either by detaining individuals who are identified and deemed to pose a risk who are currently residing in the community, or by extending the detention of those who are currently serving prison sentences, would need wide debate.

8   Future directions

Executive summary

The College accepts that offenders with personality disorder should be helped to cope in general, to modify specific behaviours, and to have their underlying disorder treated when possible. The current system in which a highly selected group receives therapeutic interventions in secure hospital units is under challenge, but any new system needs to take account of a number of factors. European targets have been set for the resolution of problems facing all disciplines, working together towards more effective diagnosis, assessment, treatment and management. There are resource issues that would make the implementation of any new system difficult. It would be senseless to focus on established personality disorder without considering primary prevention, to leap to new and unproven ideas for the sake of 'doing something', and to ignore the practical and ethical dilemmas raised by any new legislation that might be required. Above all, the need is reiterated for government-supported clinical trials in which pilot units might be monitored, or one treatment modality compared with another.

When possible, attempts should be made to help patients suffering from personality disorder to cope in general, to modify specific traits and behaviours and to change their underlying disturbance. The Royal College of Psychiatrists accepts that a subgroup of these offenders pose a risk to society and to themselves, though they are not alone in doing so. This subgroup may warrant special consideration.

The College does not believe that the solution to all these problems is to continue with the current system in which selected individuals receive therapeutic interventions in secure hospital units. However, the clarity of these assertions contrasts with the uncertainties over diagnosis, assessment, treatment and management of offenders with personality disorder to which attention has been drawn throughout this report. These uncertainties will not be relieved unless the following issues are taken into consideration.

The problems are not confined to British psychiatry. At the Third European Congress on Personality Disorders, held in Sheffield in July 1998, the 14 European countries represented identified six future targets:

(a) An internationally accepted procedure for routine assessment of personality status in all patients presenting to psychiatric services.

(b) Separate recognition of those with severe personality disorder requiring specialised interventions, using a similarly accepted procedure.

(c) The establishment, within each country, of at least one centre of excellence devoted to the study and treatment of personality disorder.

(d) The setting up of national programmes of research into personality disorder.

(e) National centres devoted to the training of all staff involved in the treatment of severe personality disorder, with the establishment of a formal qualification to achieve common standards of competence.

(f) Audit systems for the monitoring of care and treatment in all specialised services, so as to maintain those standards.

None of the tasks involved can be dealt with by mental health professionals working alone. These are multi-disciplinary issues requiring multi-disciplinary solutions, based on a consensus of aims and common commitment to training, backed by enlightened government policy.

There are critical resource implications. Despite the priority placed by the Department of Health on the severely mentally ill, secure services for offenders with severe mental illness remain inadequate. Where there are no financial resources for the establishment of their own facilities, local services must depend on extra-contractual referrals which are themselves expensive. Even where such resources are available, manpower shortages may prevent the expansion of services. In this context, it must be concluded that British psychiatry would struggle to take on a major role in any new developments for offenders with personality disorders, unless there was a significant increase in recruitment of a range of professional staff, including nurses and clinical psychologists.

The number of patients with personality disorders presenting to adult services, whatever their future configuration, could be reduced if equal attention were given to prevention strategies. It is not ethical, therapeutically logical or cost-effective to concentrate wholly on offenders with established personality disorder if the roots of their disorder can be detected and addressed at an earlier stage.

Serious antisocial behaviour in adolescents is heterogeneous in its pervasiveness, persistence, severity and pattern. Adolescent forensic services, linking with generic child and adolescent mental health services, should focus resources and interventions on those at risk. These would include:

(a) antisocial behaviour of very early onset and persistence;
(b) antisocial behaviour influenced by genetic factors, as in attention-deficit hyperactivity disorder;
(c) antisocial, and often violent, behaviour where there is an indication of altered neural function;
(d) antisocial behaviour associated with lack of remorse, absence of close relationships and apparent emotional detachment;
(e) antisocial behaviour that is an intrusive component of a wider mental disorder.

Particular attention should be given to those groups that are difficult to reach in current service formats and require the cooperation of child, adolescent and adult services, forensic and non-forensic components, and psychiatric and non-psychiatric disciplines. These include:

(a) juvenile sex offenders;
(b) substance misusers;
(c) people with learning disabilities.

The survey conduced by Cope (1993) on behalf of the Forensic Psychiatry Faculty of the Royal College of Psychiatrists exposed mixed views on how best to manage offenders with personality disorder. However, only 10% believed that such patients were untreatable; the great majority favoured multi-disciplinary approaches, and there was considerable support for setting up specialised units within the secure psychiatric system. Where offenders with personality disorder had a comorbid mental illness, their needs were not thought to be properly met by the penal system.

If thinking does not appear to have moved on from this position, and if there is no universal agreement on future changes, this is because the research evidence is not available on which to base crucial decisions. Such evidence could only come from properly conducted clinical trials involving random allocation of patients to different treatment modalities with long-term comparison of outcome. Such trials could only be conducted within a secure system and would, therefore, need the active cooperation and support of government; they cannot be the responsibility of psychiatrists alone.

Any new system for the treatment of offenders with personality disorder must rely on such proven efficacy. This is an extremely difficult group to manage; any fault-lines in the system for their care will be exposed and exploited.

The College counsels against too great a reliance on superficially attractive service models elsewhere that are not yet systematically evaluated. The Dutch system is an oft-quoted example.

The Dutch penal code contains a special provision to protect society against mentally disturbed offenders by means of compulsory psychiatric treatment. This penal measure is called *Ter Beschikking Stelling* (TBS), which can be translated as 'Disposal to be Treated on Behalf of the State'. The court may invoke this measure when an offender has committed a serious and violent criminal act with a high risk of recurrence. The measure is applied in cases where, because of a mental disturbance, the court has not held offenders to be entirely responsible for their crimes. A TBS Order is semi-indeterminate, initially for two years, but subsequently renewable by a court at one- or two-yearly intervals and can continue indefinitely. The offender is detained in a treatment institution which provides conditions of high security. When considering an extension of the Order, courts rely heavily on the opinion of those responsible for the individual's care and on their prediction of future dangerousness. However, every two years the court can request a second independent opinion concerning continued detention and this may also be requested by the offender's legal representative.

The aim has traditionally been to effect an offender's resocialisation by treatment and, thus, to protect the public. Treatment is a form of residential psychotherapy and courts are obliged to ensure that it takes place so that the Order is not merely an indefinite prison sentence. While detention is mandatory, treatment is not. However, those who repeatedly refuse treatment will risk repeated renewal of the Order. To facilitate the TBS process, there is a network of secure centres in Holland which are part of a range of services for people with personality disorder. One clinic provides a central assessment service and other clinics are primarily involved in delivering treatment. However, criticism is beginning to emerge that questions this approach and, more importantly, no formal evaluations have been made of the effectiveness of the system.

A way forward

One way forward in the UK might be to develop pilot experimental units, either within the penal system or in appropriate facilities in high security hospitals, for offenders with personality disorder. They should have an agreed and consistent initial assessment procedure, and a safe system of transfer from one therapeutic setting and one level of security to another, according to subsequent need and risk. Such units should have a strong academic base and should be the training centres for professionals working in this field.

It would not be possible to evaluate fully such units without linking them to the process of community supervision. The College recognises the need to protect the public and, therefore, the need to impose a continual process of risk assessment. However, health professionals are neither trained nor equipped with the resources to take the lead role in what may amount to community surveillance. This should be led by the probation service, which has long experience of supervising offenders in the community. This would still require considerable input from health and social services, especially where offenders have dual or treble diagnoses, involving personality disorder, substance misuse and/or concurrent mental illness. Substance misuse services might themselves require further development to support such community supervision.

The results of research in these pilot experimental units would inform the health and criminal justice systems on the way forward, on the respective roles of the penal and secure hospital systems in general, and on the responsibilities of different professions in particular. Psychiatrists would be asked to shoulder only those components of public safety for which their medical skills are shown to be of proven value. Where that is so, the skills will need to be based on adequate training and resources if psychiatrists' responsibilities are to be safely discharged.

All of the above needs to be set in a legislative context. The Mental Health Act 1983 is under review. New legislation might be required to manage offenders with personality disorder released into the community and increasing consideration is being given to reviewable sentencing powers. Under these powers, detention in prison could be extended and renewed if an individual was considered to be of high risk to public safety. That would be a decision for a court, but there is a possibility that psychiatrists would be drawn into the decision-making process. This would pose major professional and ethical dilemmas.

Recommendations and conclusions

(a) Solutions to the current uncertainties should take account of European targets, such as those set at the Sheffield Congress, 1998.

(b) These are multi-disciplinary issues that require cooperation between all the disciplines involved.

(c) Any new systems for the treatment and management of offenders with personality disorder will have resource implications. This should not be at the expense of already hard-pressed services for the severely mentally ill.

(d) Equal priority needs to be given to prevention. This entails close cooperation between generic child and adolescent mental health services, substance misuse, learning disability and adolescent forensic services and adult psychiatric services.

(e) Any new developments must be based on randomised controlled trials. These need to be resourced and supported by government.

(f) European models based on flimsy evaluation should be treated with caution.

(g) Pilot experimental units, within the penal system or high security hospitals, should be set up and researched to establish treatment efficacy.

(h) Surveillance of offenders with personality disorder released into the community would be best led by the probation service, supported by health and social services input.

(i) Any new configuration of services will have legislative implications.

9   References

ALPET, J. E. & SPILLMAN, M. K. (1997) Psychotherapeutic approaches to aggressive and violent patients. *Psychiatric Clinics in North America*, **20**, 453–472.

AMERICAN PSYCHIATRIC ASSOCIATION (1980) *Diagnostic and Statistical Manual of Mental Disorders* (3rd edn)(DSM–III). Washington, DC: APA.

—— (1987) *Diagnostic and Statistical Manual of Mental Disorders* (3rd edn, revised)(DSM–III–R). Washington, DC: APA.

—— (1994) *Diagnostic and Statistical Manual of Mental Disorders* (4th edn)(DSM–IV). Washington, DC: APA.

ANTHONY, J. E. (1987) Children at high risk for psychosis growing up successfully. In *The Invulnerable Child* (eds J. E. Anthony & B. J. Cohler). New York: Guilford Press.

ASCHENBACH, T. M. & EDELBROCK, C. S. (1981) Behavioral problems and competencies reported by parents of normal and disturbed children aged four through sixteen. *Monographs of the Society for Research in Child Development*, **46**, 1–82.

BAILEY, J. & MacCULLOCH, M. (1992*a*) Characteristics of 112 cases discharged directly to the community from a new Special Hospital and some comparisons of performance *Journal of Forensic Psychiatry*, **3**, 91–112.

—— & —— (1992*b*) Patterns of reconviction in patients discharged directly to the community from a Special Hospital: implications for after-care. *Journal of Forensic Psychiatry*, **3**, 445–461.

BEARDSLEE, W. R., BEMPORN, J., KELLER, M. B., *et al* (1983) Children of parents with major affective disorders: a review. *American Journal of Psychiatry*, **140**, 825–832.

BECK, A. T. & FREEMAN, A. (1990) *Cognitive Therapy of Personality Disorders*. New York: Guilford Press.

BERRUETA-CLEMENT, J. R., SCHWEINHART, L. J., BARNETT, W. S., *et al* (1984) *Changed Lives*. Ypsilanti, MI: High/Scope.

BLACKBURN, R. (1982) The Special Hospitals Assessment of Personality and Socialisation. Unpublished manuscript available from Department of Clinical Psychology, University of Liverpool.

—— (1992) Clinical programmes with psychopaths. In *Clinical Approaches to the Mentally Disordered Offender* (eds K. Howells & C. Hollis). Chichester: Wiley.

BLAND, R. C. (1988) Psychiatric epidemiology. *Canadian Journal of Psychiatry*, **33**, 618–625.

——, CRELLIN, M. C., MORGON, E. M., *et al* (1990) Prevalence of personality disorder in a special hospital population. *Journal of Forensic Psychiatry*, **1**, 43–52.

BLUMSTEIN, A. & COHEN, J. (1979) Estimation of individual crime rates from arrest records. *Journal of Criminal Law and Criminology*, **70**, 561–585.

—— & —— (1987) Characterising criminal careers. *Science*, **237**, 985–991.

BONTA, J., LAW, M. & HANSON, K. (1998) The prediction of criminal and violent recidivism among mentally disordered offenders: a meta-analysis. *Psychological Bulletin*, **123**, 123–142.

BORRIELLO, J. (1979) Group therapy with acting-out patients: specific problems and techniques. *American Journal of Psychotherapy*, **33**, 275–285.

Botvin, G. J., Baker, E., Dusenberry, L., *et al* (1990) Preventing adolescent drug abuse through a multimodal cognitive–behavioural approach: results of a three-year study. *Journal of Consulting and Clinical Psychology*, **58**, 437–446.

Buss, A. H. & Durkee, A. (1957) An inventory for assessing different kinds of hostility. *Journal of Consulting Psychology*, **21**, 343–348.

Carney, F. L. (1972) Some recurring therapeutic issues in group psychotherapy with criminal patients. *American Journal of Psychotherapy*, **26**, 34–41.

—— (1977) Out-patient treatment of the aggressive offender. *American Journal of Psychotherapy*, **31**, 265–274.

Casey, P. R. & Tyrer, P. J. (1986) Personality, functioning and symptomatology. *Journal of Psychiatric Research*, **20**, 363–374.

Cleckley, H. (1976) *The Mask of Sanity.* St Louis, MO: C. V. Mosby Co.

Cohler, B. J. (1987) Adversity, resilience and the study of lives. In *The Invulnerable Child* (eds J. E. Anthony & B. J. Cohler). New York: Guilford Press.

Coid, J. W. (1992) DSM–III diagnosis in criminal psychopaths: A way forward. *Criminal Behaviour and Mental Health*, **2**, 78–79.

—— (1993*a*) Current concepts and classifications of psychopathic disorder. In *Personality Disorder Reviewed* (eds P. Tyrer & G. Stein), pp. 113–164. London: Gaskell.

—— (1993*b*) An affective syndrome in psychopaths with borderline personality disorder? *British Journal of Psychiatry*, **162**, 641–650.

—— & Cordess, C. (1992) Compulsory admission of dangerous psychopaths. *British Medical Journal*, **304**, 1581–1582.

—— (1998) Axis II disorders and motivation for serious criminal behaviour. In *Psychopathology and Violent Crime* (ed. A. E. Skodol), pp. 53–98. Washington, DC: American Psychiatric Press.

Cooke, D. J. (1989) Containing violent prisoners: an analysis of Barlinnie special unit. *British Journal of Criminology*, **29**, 129–143.

—— (1994) *Psychological Disturbance in the Scottish Prison System: Prevalence, Precipitants and Policy.* Scottish Prison Service Occasional Paper No. 3. Edinburgh: Scottish Prison Service.

Cope, R. (1993) A survey of forensic psychiatrists views on psychopathic disorder. *Journal of Forensic Psychiatry*, **4**, 215–235

Cote, G. & Hodgins, S. (1990) Co-occurring mental disorders among criminal offenders. *Bulletin of the American Academy of Psychiatry and Law*, **18**, 271–281.

Dahlstrom, W. G., Welsh, G. S. & Dahlstrom, L. E. (1975) *An MMPI Handbook.* Vol. 2. Minneapolis, MN: University of Minnesota Press.

Davidson, K. & Tyrer, P. (1996) Cognitive therapy for antisocial and borderline personality disorder: single case study series. *British Journal of Clinical Psychology*, **35**, 413–429.

de Girolamo, G. & Reich, J. H. (1993) *Personality Disorders.* Geneva: World Health Organization.

Department of Health (1993) *Legal Powers on the Care of Mentally Ill People in the Community. Report of the Internal Review.* London: Department of Health.

—— (1994) *Health Services Guidelines. Guidance on the Discharge of Mentally Disordered People and their Continuing Care in the Community.* HSG(94)27. Leeds: NHS Executive.

—— (1999) *The Report of the Committee of Inquiry into the Personality Disorder Unit, Ashworth Special Hospital.* Cm 4194-II (The Fallon Inquiry). London: HMSO.

Department of Health and Social Security (1985) *Mental Illness in Hospitals and Units in England. Results from the Mental Health Inquiry Statistical Bulletin, Government Statistical Services.* London: HMSO.

Dishion, T. F., Patterson, G. R. & Kavanagh, K. A. (1992) An experimental test of the coercion model: linking theory, measurement and intervention. In *Preventing Antisocial Behaviour* (eds J. McCord & R. Tremblay), pp. 253–282. New York: Guilford Press.

DOCHERTY, J. P., FIESTER, S. J. & SHEA, T. (1986) Syndrome diagnosis and personality disorder. In *Psychiatry Update*. Vol. 5 (eds A. J. Frances & R. E. Hales), pp. 315–355. Washington, DC: American Psychiatric Press.

DOLAN, B. & COID, J. (1993) *Psychopathic and Antisocial Personality Disorders: Treatment and Research Issues*. London: Gaskell.

——, EVANS, C. & NORTON, K. (1995) Multiple Axis II diagnoses of personality disorder. *British Journal of Psychiatry*, **166**, 107–112.

——, WARREN, F. M., MENZIES, D., *et al* (1996) Cost-offset following specialist treatment of severe personality disorders. *Psychiatric Bulletin*, **20**, 413–417.

——, —— & NORTON, K. (1997) Change in borderline symptoms one year after therapeutic community treatment for severe personality disorder. *British Journal of Psychiatry*, **171**, 274–279.

DROSKIN, J. A. & STEADMAN, H. J. (1994) Using intensive care management to reduce violence by mentally ill persons in the community. *Hospital and Community Psychiatry*, **45**, 679–684.

EASTMAN, N. (1997) The Mental Health (Patients in the Community) Act 1995. A clinical analysis. *British Journal of Psychiatry*, **170**, 492–496.

FALCONER, M. A. & SHUR, P. (1959) Surgical treatment of mental illness. In *Recent Progress in Psychiatry*. New York: Grove Press.

FARRINGTON, D. P. (1993) Understanding and preventing bullying. In *Crime and Justice*, vol. 17 (eds M. Tonry & N. Morris), pp. 381–458. Chicago, IL: University of Chicago Press.

—— (1997) Evaluating a community crime prevention programmes. *Evaluation*, **3**, 157–173.

FIRST, M. B., SPITZER, R. L., GIBBON, M., *et al* (1995) The Structured Clinical Interview for DSM–III–R Personality Disorders (SCID–II): Part 1: Description. *Journal of Personality Disorders*, **9**, 83–91.

FITCH, W. L. (1998) Sex offender commitment in the United States. *Journal of Forensic Psychiatry*, **9**, 237–240.

GARMEZY, N. (1983) Stressors in childhood. In *Stress, Coping and Development in Children* (eds N. Garmezy & M. Rutter). New York: McGraw-Hill.

—— (1985) Broadening research on developmental risk. Implications for studies of vulnerable and stress resistant children. In *Early Identification of Children at Risk* (eds W. F. Frankenburg, R. M. Einde & J. W. Sullivan). New York: Plenum Press.

GENDREAU, P. & ROSS, R. R. (1979) Effective correctional treatment: Bibliotherapy for cynics. *Crime and Delinquency*, **4**, 349–407.

—— & —— (1987) Revivification of rehabilitation: evidence from the 1980s. *Justice Quarterly*, **4**, 349–407.

GOVERNMENT STATISTICAL SERVICE (1991) Inpatients formally detained in hospital under the Mental Health Act 1983 and other legislations, England, 1984–1988/9. *Statistical Bulletin*, **2**, 91.

GROUNDS, A. T. (1987) Detention of 'psychopathic disorder' patients in special hospitals: critical issues. *British Journal of Psychiatry*, **151**, 474–478.

GUEST, J. S, HART, W. N., COOKSON, R. S., *ET AL* (1996) Pharmaco-economic evaluation of long-term treatment with risperidone for patients with chronic schizophrenia. *British Journal of Medical Economics*, **10**, 59–67.

GUNN, J. & ROBERTSON, G. (1976) Psychopathic personality: a conceptual problem. *Psychological Medicine*, **6**, 631–634.

HAMILTON, J. (1990) Special hospitals and the state hospital. In *Principles and Practice of Forensic Psychiatry* (eds R. Bluglass & P. Bowden), pp. 1363–1373. Edinburgh: Churchill Livingstone.

HANN, R. G., HARMAN, W. G. & PEASE, K. (1991) Does parole reduce the risk of reconviction? *Howard Journal*, **30**, 66–75.

Hare, E. H. (1980) A research scale for the assessment of psychopathy in criminal populations. *Personality and Individual Differences*, 1, 111–117.

—— (1983) Diagnosis of antisocial personality disorder in two prison populations. *American Journal of Psychiatry*, 140, 887–890.

—— (1991) *The Hare Psychopathy Checklist – Revised*. Toronto: Multi-Health Systems.

Harris, G. T. & Rice, M. E. (1984) Mentally disordered firesetters: psychodynamic versus empirical approaches. *International Journal of Law and Psychiatry*, 7, 19–34.

Hawkins, J. D., Doueck, H. J. & Lishner, D. M. (1988) Changing teaching practices in mainstream classrooms to improve bonding and behaviour of low achievers. *American Educational Research Journal*, 25, 31–50.

——, Von Cleve, E. & Catalano, R. F., Jr (1991) Reducing early childhood aggression: results of a primary prevention program. *Journal of the American Academy of Child and Adolescent Psychiatry*, 30, 208–217.

—— & Catalano, R. F. (1992) *Communities that Care*. San Francisco, CA: Jossey-Bass.

——, —— & Miller, J. Y. (1992a) Risk and protective factors for alcohol and other drug problems in adolescence and early adulthood: Implications for substance abuse prevention. *Psychological Bulletin*, 112, 64–105.

——, ——, Morrison, D. M., *et al* (1992b) The Seattle social development project: effects of the first four years on protective factors and problem behaviours. In *Preventive Antisocial Behaviour* (eds J. McCord & R. Tramblay), pp. 139–161. New York: Guilford Press.

Hechtman, L. (1991) Resilience and vulnerability in long-term outcome of attention deficit hyperactive disorder. *Canadian Journal of Psychiatry*, 36, 415–421.

Herbert, M. (1987) *Conduct Disorders of Childhood and Adolescence: a Social Learning Perspective* (2nd edn). Chichester: Wiley.

Hesselbrock, M. N. (1986) Childhood behaviour problems and adult antisocial personality disorder in alcoholism. In *Psychopathology and Addictive Disorders* (ed. R. E. Myer). New York: Guilford Press.

Hirschi, T. & Gottfredson, M. (1983) Age and the explanation of crime. *American Journal of Sociology*, 89, 552–584.

Hollin, C. R. (1986) *Cognitive–Behavioural Interventions with Young Offenders*. Elmsfor, NY: Pergamon Press.

Hollon, S. D., Kendall, P. C. & Lumry, A. (1986) Specificity of depressogenic cognitions in clinical depression. *Journal of Abnormal Psychology*, 95, 52–59.

Hyler, S. E. (1994) *Personality Diagnostic Questionnaire – 4*. New York: New York State Psychiatric Institute.

—— & Reider, R. O. (1984) *Personality Diagnostic Questionnaire – Revised*. New York: New York State Psychiatric Institute.

Institute of Medicine (1989) *Research on Children and Adolescents with Mental, Behavioural and Developmental Disorders*. Washington, DC: National Academic Press.

Jew, C. C., Clanon, T. L. & Mattocks, A. L. (1972) The effectiveness of group psychotherapy in a correctional institution. *American Journal of Psychiatry*, 129, 602–605.

Jordan, B. K., Schlenger, W. E, Fairbank, J. A., *et al* (1996) Prevalence of psychiatric disorders among incarcerated women. II. Convicted felons entering prison. *Archives of General Psychiatry*, 53, 513–519.

Kass, F., Skodol, A. E., Charles, E., *et al* (1985) Scaled ratings of DSM–III personality disorders. *American Journal of Psychiatry*, 143, 627–630.

Kazdin, A. E. (1987) Treatment of antisocial behaviour in children: current status and future directions. *Psychological Bulletin*, 102, 187–203.

—— (1993) Adolescent mental health. Prevention and treatment programs. *American Journal of Psychology*, 48, 127–141

——, Siegel, T. C. & Bass, D. (1992) Cognitive problem-solving skills training and parent management training in the treatment of antisocial behaviour in children. *Journal of Consulting Clinical Psychology*, 60, 733–747.

KELLAM, S. G., ENSMINGER, M. E. & TURNER, R. J. (1977) Family structure and the mental health of children. Concurrent and longitudinal community wide studies. *Archives of General Psychiatry*, **34**, 1012–1022.

KERNBERG, O. F. (1975) *Borderline Conditions and Pathological Narcissism*. New York: Jason Aronson.

—— (1984) *Severe Personality Disorders: Psychotherapeutic Strategies*. New Haven, CT: Yale University Press.

KOHUT, H. (1975) *The Restoration of the Self*. New York: International Universities Press.

KROLL, J. L., CAREY, K. S. & SINES, L. K. (1985) Twenty year follow-up of borderline personality disorde: a pilot study. In *IV World Congress of Biological Psychiatry*, vol. 7 (ed. C. Shangass), pp. 577–579. New York: Elsevier.

LALLY, J. R., MANGIONE, P. L. & HONIG, A. S. (1988) Long-range impact of an early intervention with low-income children and their families. In *Parent Education as Early Childhood Intervention* (ed. D. Power), pp. 79–104. Norwood, NJ: Ablex.

LANGAN, P. A. & GREENFELD, L. A. (1983) *Career Patterns in Crime*. (Bureau of Criminal Statistics Special Report NCJ-88672.) Washington, DC: Bureau of Justice Statistics.

LEBLANC, M. & FRECHETTE, M. (1989) *Male Criminal Activity from Childhood through Youth. Multilevel and Developmental Perspectives*. New York: Springer-Verlag.

LEONHARD, K. (1968) *Akzentuierte Personlichkeiten*. Berlin: Verlag Volk und Gesundheit.

LEWIS, D. O., LOVELEY, R., YEAGER, C., *et al* (1989) Towards a therory of the genesis of violence: a follow-up study of delinquents. *Journal of the American Academy of Child and Adolescent Psychiatry*, **28**, 431–436.

LEWIS, G. & APPLEBY, L.(1988) Personality disorder: the patients that psychiatrists dislike. *British Journal of Psychiatry*, **153**, 44–49.

LIVESLEY, W. J. (1986) Trait and behavioral prototypes of personality disorder. *American Journal of Psychiatry*, **143**, 728–732.

—— (1991) Classifying personality disorders: ideal types, prototypes, or dimensions? *Journal of Personality Disorders*, **5**, 52–59.

—— & JACKSON, D. N.(1993) The internal consistency and factorial structures of behaviors judged to be associated with DSM–III personality disorders. *American Journal of Psychiatry*, **143**, 1473–1474.

LOEBER, R. (1982) The stability of antisocial and delinquent child behavior: a review. *Child Development*, **53**, 1431–1446.

——, LAHEY, B. B. & THOMAS, C. (1991) Diagnostic conundrum of oppositional defiant disorder and conduct disorder. *Journal of Abnormal Psychology*, **100**, 379–390.

LORANGER, A. W., SUSMAN, V. L., OLDHAM, M. M., *et al* (1987) The Personality Disorder Examination: a preliminary report. *Journal of Personality Disorders*, **1**, 1–13.

——, SARTORIUS, N., ANDREOLI, A., *et al* (1994) The International Personality Disorder Examination: the WHO/ADAMHA international pilot study of personality disorders. *Archives of General Psychiatry*, **51**, 215–224.

MACCULLOCH, M. & BAILEY, J. (1993) Issues in the management and rehabilitation of patients in maximum secure hospitals. *Journal of Forensic Psychiatry*, **4**, 25–44.

MCCORD, J. (1982) A longitudinal view of the relationship between paternal absence and crime. In *Abnormal Offenders, Delinquency and the Criminal Justice System* (eds J. Gunn & D. P. Farrington). Chichester: Wiley.

MCCORD, W. & MCCORD, J. (1964) *The Psychopath: An Essay on the Criminal Mind*. Princeton, NJ: Van Nostrand.

MCGLASHAN, T. H. (1986) Long-term outcome of borderline patients. *Archives of General Psychiatry*, **40**, 20–30.

MADEN, A., CURLE, C., MEUX, C., *et al* (1993) The treatment and security needs of patients in special hospitals. *Criminal Behaviour and Mental Health*, **3**, 290–306.

MAIER , W., LICHTERMAN, D., KLINGER, T., *et al* (1992) Prevalence of personality disorders (DSM–III–R) in the community. *Journal of Personality Disorders*, **6**, 187–196.

MANN, A. H., JENKINS, R., CUTTING, J. C., *et al* (1981) The development and use of a standardized assessment of abnormal personality. *Psychological Medicine*, **11**, 839–847.

MENZIES, R., DOLAN, B. & NORTON, K. (1993) Are short-term savings worth long-term costs. *Psychiatric Bulletin*, **17**, 517–519.

MILLON, T. & DAVIS, R. D. (1994) Millon's evolutionary model of normal and abnormal personality: theory and measures. In *Differentiating Normal and Abnormal Personality* (eds S. Strack & M. Lorr), pp. 79–113. New York: Springer.

—, — & MILLON, C. (1997) *MCMI–III Manual*. Minneapolis, MN: National Computer Systems.

MORAN, P. (1999) *Antisocial Personality Disorder: An Epidemiological Perspective*. London: Gaskell.

MURRAY, D. M., LEUPKER, R. V., JOHNSON, C. A., *et al* (1984) The prevention of cigarette smoking in children: a comparison of four strategies. *Journal of Applied Social Psychology*, **14**, 274–288.

NESTADT, G., ROMANOSKI, A. J., CHAHAL, R., *et al* (1990) An epidemilogical study of histrionic personality disorder. *Psychological Medicine*, **20**, 413–422.

—, EATON, W. W., ROMANOSKI, A. J., *et al* (1994) Assessment of DSM–III personality structure in a general-population survey. *Comprehensive Psychiatry*, **35**, 54–63.

—, ROMANOSKI, A. J., BROWN, C. H., *et al* (1991) DSM–III compulsive personality disorder: an epidemiological survey. *Psychological Medicine*, **21**, 461–471.

—, —, SAMUELS, J. F., *et al* (1992) The relationship between personality and DSM–III axis I disorders in the population: results from an epidemiological survey. *American Journal of Psychiatry*, **149**, 1228–1233.

OFFORD, D. R. (1982) Family backgrounds of male and female delinquents. In *Abnormal Offenders, Delinquency and the Criminal Justice System* (eds J. Gunn & D. P. Farrington), pp. 129–151. Chichester: Wiley.

OLDHAM, J. M. & SKODOL, A. E. (1991) Personality disorders in the public sector. *Hospital and Community Psychiatry*, **42**, 481–487.

—, —, KELLMAN, H. D., *et al* (1992) Diagnosis of DSM–III–R personality disorders by two semistructured interviews: patterns of comorbidity. *American Journal of Psychiatry*, **149**, 213–220.

OLDS, D. L., HENDERSON, C. R., CHAMBERLAIN, R., *ET AL* (1986*a*) Preventing child abuse and neglect: A randomised trial of nurse home visitation. *Paediatrics*, **78**, 65–78.

—, —, TATELBAUM, R., *ET AL* (1986*b*) Improving the delivery of prenatal care and outcomes of pregnancy: A randomised trial of nurse home visitation. *Paediatrics*, **77**, 16–28.

OLIVER, J. E. (1988) Successive generations of child maltreatment. The children. *British Journal of Psychiatry*, **153**, 543–553.

— & BUCHANAN, A. H. (1979) Generations of maltreated children and multiagency care in one kindred. *British Journal of Psychiatry*, **135**, 289–303.

OLWEUS, D. (1993) *Bullying at School*. Oxford: Blackwell.

— (1994) Bullying at school: basic facts and effects of a school-based intervention program. *Journal of Child Psychology and Psychiatry*, **35**, 1171–1190.

PALMER, T. (1992) *The Re-Emergence of Correctional Intervention*. Newbury Park, CA: Sage.

PARIS, J., BROWN, R. & KNOWLIS, D. (1987) Long-term follow-up of borderline patients in a general hospital. *Comprehensive Psychiatry*, **28**, 530–535.

—, KNOWLIS, D. & BROWN, R. (1988) Developmental factors in the outcome of BPD. In *Proceedings and Summary, 141st Annual Meeting of the American Psychiatric Association*, p. 157. Washington, DC: American Psychiatric Association.

PATTERSON, G. R. (1982) *A Social Learning Approach, Volume 3: Coercive Familt Processes*. New York: Castalia.

—, REID, J. B. & DISHION, T. J. (1992) *Antisocial Boys*. Eugene, OR: Castalia.

PETERSILIA, J., GREENWOOD, P. W. & LAVIN, M. (1978) *Criminal Careers of Habitual Felons.* Washington, DC: US Government Printing Office.

PETERSON, M. A. & BRAIKER, H. B. (1980) *Doing Crime: A Survey of California Prison Inmates.* Santa Monica, CA: RAND.

PFOHL, B., BLUM, N. & ZIMMERMAN, M. (1995) *Structured Interview for DSM–IV Personality: SIDP–IV.* Iowa, IA: Department of Psychiatry, University of Iowa.

PLAKUN, E. M., BURKHARDT, P. E. & MULLER, J. P. (1985) Fourteen-year follow-up of borderline and schizotypal personality disorders. *Comprehensive Psychiatry,* **26**, 448–455.

QUINTON, D. & RUTTER, M. (1984) Parenting behaviour of mothers raised 'in care'. In *Longitudinal Studies in Child Psychology and Psychiatry: Practical Lessons from Research Experience.* Chichester: Wiley.

RAE-GRANT, N., THOMAS, B. H., OFFORD, D. R., *et al* (1989) Risk, protective factors and the prevalence of behavioural and emotional disorders in children and adolescents. *Journal of the American Academy of Child and Adolescent Psychiatry,* **28**, 262–268.

RECKLESS, J. B. (1970) Enforced out-patient treatment of advantaged pseudosociopathic neurotically disturbed young women. *Canadian Psychiatric Association Journal,* **15**, 335–345.

REICH, J. (1992) Measurement of DSM–III and DSM–III–R borderline personality disorder. In *Borderline Personality Disorder: Clinical and Empirical Perspectives* (eds. J. F. Clarkin, E. Marziali & H. Munroe-Blum), pp. 114–148. New York: Guilford Press.

——, YATES, W. & NDUAGUBA, M. (1989) Prevalence of DSM–III personality disorders in the community. *Social Psychiatry and Psychiatric Epidemiology,* **24**, 12–16.

—— & DE GIROLAMO, G. (1997) Epidemiology of DSM–III personality disorders in the community and in clinical populations. In *Assessment and Diagnosis of Personality Disorders. The ICD–10 International Personality Disorder Examination (IPDE)* (eds A. W. Loranger, A. Janca & M. Sartorius), pp. 18–42. Cambridge: Cambridge University Press.

REICH, W. (1949) *Character Analysis.* New York: Orgone Institute Press.

RICE, M. E. & HARRIS, G. T. (1995) Violent recidivism: assessing predictive validity. *Journal of Consulting and Clinical Psychology,* **63**, 737–748.

ROBERTSON, G. (1989) Treatment for offending patients: how should success be measured? *Medicine, Science and the Law,* **29**, 303–307.

—— (1992) Objections to the present system. *Criminal Behaviour and Mental Health,* **2**, 114–123.

ROBINS, L. N. (1966) *Deviant Children Grown Up.* Baltimore, MD: Williams & Wilkins.

—— (1970) Follow-up studies of childhood conduct disorder. In *Psychiatric Epidemiology* (eds E. Hare & J. Wing). London: Oxford University Press.

—— (1978) Sturdy childhood predictors of adult antisocial behaviour: replications from longitudinal studies. *Psychological Medicine,* **8**, 611–622.

—— (1981) Epidemiological approaches to natural history research: antisocial disorders in children. *Journal of the American Academy of Child Psychiatry,* **20**, 556–580.

—— & MCEVOY, L. T. (1990) Conduct problems as predictors of substance abuse. In *Straight and Devious Pathways to Adulthood* (eds L. N. Robins & M. R. Rutter). Cambridge: Cambridge University Press.

—— & PRICE, R. K. (1991) Adult disorders predicted by childhood conduct problems: results from the NIMH Epidemiologic Catchment Area project. *Psychiatry,* **54**, 116–132.

——, TIPP, P. & PRZYBECK, T. (1991) Antisocial personality. In *Psychiatric Disorder in America. The ECA study* (eds L. N. Robins & D. Regier), pp. 258–290. New York: Free Press.

ROSS, D. R., LEWIN, R., GOLD, K., *et al* (1988) The psychiatric uses of cold wet sheet packs. *American Journal of Psychiatry,* **145**, 242–245.

ROSS, R. R. & ROSS, B. D. (1988) Delinquency prevention through cognitive training. *New Education,* **10**, 70–75.

ROYAL COLLEGE OF PSYCHIATRISTS SPECIAL WORKING PARTY ON CLINICAL ASSESSMENT AND MANAGEMENT OF RISK (1996) *Assessment and Clinical Management of Risk of Harm to Other People.* Council Report CR53. London: Royal College of Psychiatrists

RUTTER, M. (1979) Protective factors in childrens responses to stress and disadvantage. In *Primary Prevention of Psychopathology*, Vol. 3 (eds M. W. Kent & J. E. Rolf). Hanover, NH: University Press of New England.

—— (1985) Resilience in the face of adversity: protective factors and resistance to psychiatric disorder. *British Journal of Psychiatry*, **147**, 598–611.

—— (1987) Temperament, personality and personality disorder. *British Journal of Psychiatry*, **150**, 443–458.

—— (1989) Pathways from childhood to adult life. *Journal of Child Psychology and Psychiatry*, **30**, 23–51.

——, COX, A., TUPLING, C., *et al* (1975) Attainment and adjustment in two geographical areas: 1. The prevalence of psychiatric disorder. *British Journal of Psychiatry*, **126**, 493–509.

—— & GILLER, H. (1983) *Juvenile Delinquency: Trends and Perspectives.* London: Harmondsworth.

—— & QUINTON, D. (1984) Parental psychiatric disorder: effects on children. *Psychological Medicine*, **14**, 853–880.

RYDELIUS, P. A. (1988) The development of antisocial behaviour and sudden violent death. *Acta Psychiatrica Scandinavica*, **77**, 398–403.

SAMUELS, J. F., NESTADT, G., ROMANOSKI, A. J., *et al* (1994) DSM–III personality disorders in the community. *American Journal of Psychiatry*, **151**, 1055–1062.

SCHWEINHART, L. J. & WEIKART, D. P. (1980) *Young Children Grow Up.* Ypsilanti, MI: High/Scope.

——, BARNES, H. V. & WEIKART, D. P. (1993) *Significant Benefits.* Ypsilanti, MI: High/Scope.

SCOTTISH HOME AND HEALTH DEPARTMENT (1977) *Report of a Public Local Inquiry into the Circumstances Surrounding the Escape of Two Patients on 30 November 1976 and into Security and Other Arrangements at the Hospital.* Edinburgh: HMSO.

SINGLETON, N., MELTZER, H., GATWARD, R., *et al* (1998) *Psychiatric Morbidity Among Prisoners in England and Wales.* London: Statistical Office.

SKODOL, A. E., ROSNICK, L., KELLMAN, D., *et al* (1988) Validating structured DSM–III–R personality disorder assessments with longitudinal data. *American Journal of Psychiatry*, **145**, 1297–1299.

SMITH, D. R., SMITH, W. R. & NOMA, E. (1984) Delinquent career lines: a conceptual link between theory and juvenile offences. *Sociological Quarterly*, **25**, 155–172.

——, CORNELIUS, J., ANSELM, G., *ET AL* (1993) Efficacy of phenelzine and haloperidol in borderline personality disorder. *Archives of General Psychiatry*, **50**, 377–385.

SMITH, R. (1984) *Prison Health Care.* London: British Medical Association.

SOLOFF, P. H. (1994) Is there any drug treatment of choice for the borderline patient? *Acta Psychiatrica Scandinavica*, **89** (suppl. 379), 50–55.

——, GEORGE, A., NATHAN R. S., *et al* (1986) Progress in pharmacotherapy of personality disorders: a double blind study of amitriptyline, haloperidol and placebo. *Archives of General Psychiatry*, **43**, 691–697.

——, CORNELIUS, J., GEORGE, A., *et al* (1993) Efficacy of phenelzine and haloperidol in borderline personality disorder. *Archives of General Psychiatry*, **50**, 377–385.

SMITH, P. K. & SHARP, S. (1994) *School Bullying.* London: Routledge.

SPITZER, R. L. & WILLIAMS, J. B. W. (1987) *Structured Clinical Interview for DSM–III–R Personality Disorders (SCID–II).* New York: New York State Psychiatric Institute.

STEIN, E. & BROWN, J. D. (1991) Group therapy in a forensic setting. *Canadian Journal of Psychiatry*, **36**, 718–722.

STONE, M. H. (1990) *The Fate of Borderline Patients.* New York: Guilford Press.

STRASBURGER, L. (1986) The treatment of antisocial syndromes: the therapist's feelings. In *Unmasking the Psychopath* (eds W. Reid, J. Walker & J. Bonner), pp. 191–207. New York: Norton.

SYMINGTON, N. (1980) The response aroused by the psychopath. *International Review of Psychoanalysis*, **7**, 291–298.

TELCH, M. J., KILLEN, J. D., MCALISTER, A. L., *ET AL* (1982) Long-term follow-up of a pilot project on smoking prevention with adolescents. *Journal of Behavioural Medicine*, **5**, 1–8.

TEPLIN, L. A., ABRAM, K. M. & MCCLELLAND, G. M. (1996) Prevalence of psychiatric disorders among incarcerated women. I. Pretrial jail detainees. *Archives of General Psychiatry*, **53**, 505–512.

TOBLER, N. S. (1986) Meta-analysis of 143 drug treatment programmes: Quantitative outcome results of programme participants compared to a control or comparison group. *Journal of Drug Issues*, **16**, 537–567.

TONRY, M. & FARRINGTON, D. P. (1995) Strategic approaches to crime prevention. In *Building a Safer Society: Strategic Approaches to Crime Prevention* (eds M. Tonry & D. P. Farrington), pp. 1–20. Chicago, IL: University of Chicago Press.

TREMBLAY, R. E., LOEBER, R. & GAGNON, C. (1991) Disruptive boys with stable and unstable high fighting bahavior patterns during junior elementary school. *Journal of Abnormal Child Psychology*, **19**, 285–300.

——, VITARO, F., BERTRAND, L., *et al* (1992) Parent and child training to prevent early onset of delinquency: the Montreal longitudinal experimental study. In *Preventing Antisocial Behaviour* (eds J. McCord & R. Tremblay), pp. 117–138. New York: Guilford.

TYRER, P., ALEXANDER, M. S., CICCHETTI, D., *et al* (1979) Reliability of a schedule for rating personality disorders. *British Journal of Psychiatry*, **135**, 168–174.

—— & JOHNSON, T. (1996) Establishing the severity of personality disorder. *American Journal of Psychiatry*, **153**, 1593–1597.

VIELMA, M., VINCENTE, B., HAYES, G., *et al* (1993) Mentally abnormal homicide: a review of a special hospital male population. *Medicine, Science and the Law*, **33**, 47–54.

WALKER, N. & MCCABE, S. (1973) *Crime and Insanity in England, Volume 2: New Solutions and New Problems*. Edinburgh: Edinburgh University Press.

WALTERS, G. D. (1990) *The Criminal Lifestyle. Patterns of Serious Criminal Conduct*. Newbury Park, CA: Sage.

WELLS, J. E., BUSHNELL, J. A., HORNBLOW, A. R., *et al* (1989) Christchurch Psychiatric Epidemiology Study, Part 1: Methodology and lifetime prevalence for specific psychiatric disorders. *Australian and New Zealand Journal of Psychiatry*, **23**, 315–326.

WERNER, E. E. (1985) Stress and protective factors in children's lives. In *Longitudinal Studies in Child Psychology and Psychiatry* (ed. A. R. Nicol). Chichester: Wiley.

——, BIERMAN, J. & FRENCH, E. E. (1971) *The Children of Kauai: A Longitudinal Study from the Prenatal Period to Age Ten*. Honolulu, HI: University of Hawaii Press.

—— & SMITH, R. S. (1977) *Kauai's Children Come of Age*. Honolulu, HI: University of Hawaii Press.

—— & SMITH, R. S. (1982) *Vulnerable but Invincible: A Study of Resilient Children*. New York: McGraw-Hill.

WEST, D. J. (1969) *Present Conduct and Future Deliquency*. London: Heinmann.

—— (1982) *Delinquency: Its Roots, Careers and Prospects*. London: Heinemann.

WEST, D. J. & FARRINGTON, D. P. (1973) *Who Becomes Delinquent?* London: Heinemann.

—— & —— (1977) *The Delinquent Way of Life: Third Report of the Cambridge Study in Delinquent Development*. London: Heinemann.

WOLFGANG, M., FIGLIO, R. F. & SELLIN, T. (1972) *Delinquency in a Birth Cohort*. Chicago, IL: University of Chicago Press.

WOODY, G. E., MCLELLAN, A. T., LUBORSKY, L., *et al* (1985). Sociopathy and psychotherapy outcome. *Archives of General Psychiatry*, **42**, 1081–1086.

WORLD HEALTH ORGANIZATION (1992) *The Tenth Revision of the International Classification of Diseases and Related Disorders* (ICD–10). Geneva: World Health Organization.

YALOM, I. (1975) *The Theory and Practise of Group Psychotherapy.* New York: Basic Books.

ZANARINI, M. C., FRANKENBURG, F. R., SICKEL, A. E., *et al* (1994) *Diagnostic Interview for DSM–IV Personality Disorders (DIPD–IV).*

ZIMMERMAN, M. (1994) Diagnosing personality disorders. A review of issues and research methods. *Archives of General Psychiatry*, **51**, 225–245.

—— & CORYELL, W. (1989) DSM–III personality disorder diagnoses in a nonpatient sample; demographic correlates and comorbidity. *Archives of General Psychiatry*, **46**, 682–689.

Index

Compiled by CAROLINE SHEARD